Peter Pan

The British Musical

Book, music and lyrics by
Piers Chater-Robinson

Based on the novel by
J.M.Barrie

Samuel French — London
New York - Toronto - Hollywood

This edition was reprinted in 2003, with minor amendments to the text.

CHARACTERS

Nana, the children's pet dog and nursemaid
Wendy
John
Michael
Mr Darling
Mrs Darling
Peter Pan
Liza, the Darlings' servant

The Lost Boys:
Tootles
Nibs
Slightly
Curly
The Twins

The Pirates:
Captain Hook
Smee
Cecco
Bill Jukes
Cookson
Starkey
Skylights
Noodler
Mullins

The Indians:
Tiger Lily, a squaw
Chief
Running Dog
Cunning Fox
Bald Eagle
Stalking Deer
Grizzly Bear
Singing Bull

The Crocodile

SYNOPSIS OF SCENES

Time — Late Victorian era

MUSIC NUMBERS

1   **Overture**

ACT I

2	**The Darlings**	Mr and Mrs Darling, Wendy, John and Michael
2A	Instrumental	
3	Instrumental	
4	**Peter**	Wendy
5	Instrumental	
5A	Instrumental	
6	Instrumental	
7	**What Happens When You're Grown Up?**	Peter
8	**Come Away, Come Away**	Peter and Wendy
9A-C	Instrumental	
10	**Come Away, Come Away** (Reprise)	Peter, Wendy, John and Michael

---

Alternative ending to Act I

9 D-G	Instrumental	
10A	**Come Away, Come Away** (Reprise)	Peter, Wendy, John and Michael

---

11   **Entr'acte**

ACT II

12	**Pirates' Song**	Pirates
13	**Rich, Damp Cake**	Hook and Pirates
14	**The Crocodile's Tune** (Instrumental)	
15	Instrumental	
15A	Instrumental	
16	**Wendy's Song** (Part One)	Wendy and the Lost Boys
17	**Wendy's Song** (Part Two)	Wendy and the Lost Boys

18	Instrumental	
19	**I've Got a Funny Feeling**	Hook and Peter
20A-B	Instrumental	

Interval

21	Instrumental	
21A	Instrumental	
21B	Instrumental	
22	**Braves to War**	Indians
23	**War Dance**	Indians
24	Instrumental	
25	**Why?**	Peter and Wendy
26	**Fight Music** (Instrumental)	
26B	**Capture** (Instrumental)	
27	**Goodbye Peter Pan**	Hook
28	**You Gotta Believe**	Peter
29	Instrumental	

ACT III

30	**Pirates' Song: Avast Belay**	Pirates
31	Instrumental	
31A	Instrumental	
32	**Pirates' Song** (Reprise)	Pirates
33	**Fight Music** (Instrumental)	
34	**Fanfare** (Instrumental)	
35	**We're Going Home**	Wendy, John, Michael and the Lost Boys
36	**Peter** (Reprise)	Wendy
36A	**Instrumental**	
36B	**Instrumental**	
37	**Instrumental**	
38	**Instrumental**	
39	**The Darlings** (Reprise)	Mr and Mrs Darling, Wendy, John and Michael
40	**Don't Say Goodbye**	Peter
41	**Curtain Calls** (Instrumental)	
42	**You've Gotta Believe** (Reprise)	Full Company

The Piano/Vocal Score, and associated orchestral parts, are available on hire from Samuel French Ltd.

PRODUCTION NOTES

Flying Sequence
There are two possible ways of dealing with the flying sequences.
1. By the use of harness and wire and spots. The children can attach the wires to themselves while hiding from Liza.
2. By the use of ultra-violet light on a totally darkened stage. Only the fluorescent costumes of Peter and the children are picked up and glow as they are carried across the stage by figures dressed in black.

Suggested doubling in the cast

Mr Darling/Captain Hook (this is traditional)
Nana/Crocodile (unless a mechanical crocodile is used)
Liza/Tiger Lily
Cecco/Indian Chief
Bill Jukes/Running Dog
Cookson/Stalking Deer
Starkey/Cunning Fox
Skylights/Bald Eagle
Noodler/Grizzly Bear
Mullins/Singing Bull

ACT I

Music 1: Overture

As the House Lights dim, introductory music begins and eventually swells as the CURTAIN *rises*

SCENE 1

The children's bedroom in the Darling household

It is a very pleasant, cosy children's bedroom of the late Victorian era. There is colourful wallpaper and a warm glow from the gas lamps. In the room are three beds, a chest of drawers, a dog's kennel and a mantelpiece over the fireplace, together with other dressing. A door UL *leads to the bathroom, there is a large window in the back wall and a door* L *leads to the rest of the house*

Wendy, aged thirteen or fourteen, and John, aged twelve, are playing "he" and giggling, R. *They are dressed in night attire*

Nana, a large dog — usually a St Bernard — and the children's nursemaid, enters with seven-year-old Michael, also in night attire, on her back. They make for the bathroom

Michael (*protesting*) I won't go to bed. I won't, I won't, Nana. It isn't six o'clock yet. Two more minutes, please? One minute more? Oh dear, oh dear. I shan't love you any more, Nana. I tell you I won't be bathed, I won't, I won't!

Mrs Darling enters. She is wearing an evening dress and is looking quite beautiful

Mrs Darling Goodness me, Michael! What a lot of fuss you're making. Now be a good boy and do what Nana tells you. (*She turns to Wendy and John*) Come on, you two. Get ready for bed. Oh deary me. I wish I wasn't going out tonight. I really do.

Michael and Nana disappear into the bathroom

*Mr Darling enters like a tornado. He is in evening dress but is carrying his
white bow tie*

Mr Darling That is it; that is the last straw! I have had enough! (*He sits down
crossly on a bed*)
Wendy Why, what is the matter, Father dear?
Mr Darling Matter! The matter! This tie is the matter! IT WILL NOT TIE!
Not round my neck! Round the bedpost, oh yes! Twenty times have I made
it up round the bedpost, but round my neck, no! Oh dear no, begs to be
excused!

Mrs Darling stifles a laugh

I warn you of this, Mary, that unless this tie is round my neck we don't go
out to dinner tonight, and if I don't go out to dinner tonight, I never go to
the office again, and if I don't go to the office again you and I starve, and
our children will be flung into the streets.

*Everyone laughs at Mr Darling — he is being over-dramatic again. The
orchestra plays the introduction to Music 2 — "The Darlings"*

Nana enters from the bathroom with Michael on her back

Music 2: The Darlings

Mr Darling (*speaking*)
            The situation is becoming quite desperate
            I'm completely at my wits end
            However hard I try
            I can't tie this wretched tie
(*Singing*)   And it's sending me quietly round the bend.
            My dearest, there's something I will promise
            Though I don't give in without a fight
            But unless it's round my neck
            In less than half a sec
            We DON'T go out to dinner tonight!
Wendy   Oh Father ...
Mrs Darling ⎫ We are the Darlings
Children ⎭ Everyone a Darling
            It's the title of our family,
            And it's hard to ascertain
            Quite where we got the name
Wendy   I'm just a Darling! That's me.
All except   Yes we are the Darlings

Mr Darling   Remember we're the Darlings
(To Mrs Darling) But there's no cause to make a fuss
               For as people walk our way
               We are very proud to say
               We're the Darlings; that's us!

The orchestra continues playing

Mrs Darling *(speaking)* George dear, you're getting all upset; you know it's not good for you. Now calm down.

Mrs Darling continues as Mr Darling paces about the room, crossly

(Speaking)   If you take life just a bit slower
               Don't get excited; try to stand still.
               If you slowly count to three
               You very soon will see
(Singing)   Your mountain problem is just a molehill.
               My dearest, if you hand me your tie.

He does so

               I promise the battle will be won.

Musical interlude as she ties it

               There's no need to stamp and shout
               We'll enjoy our evening out
(Speaking)   There you are, no sooner said than done.
               Chorus
Children   ⎫ Oh we are the Darlings
Mrs Darling ⎬ Everyone a Darling
               It's the title of our family
               And it's hard to ascertain
               Quite where we got the name.
Mr Darling I'm just a Darling! That's me!
All   Oh we are the Darlings
               Just remember we're the Darlings
               So there's no cause to make a fuss
               And as people walk our way
               We're very proud to say
               We're the Darlings; that's us!

They all sing "Oh" in harmony, the sound building. Nana howls in tune ...
almost. They repeat the chorus

	Chorus
Children ⎤	Oh we are the Darlings
Mrs Darling ⎦	Everyone a Darling
	It's the title of our family
	And it's hard to ascertain
	Quite where we got the name.
Michael	I'm just a Darling! That's me!
All	Oh we are the Darlings
	Just remember we're the Darlings
	So there's no cause to make a fuss
	And as people walk our way
	We're very proud to say
	We're the Darlings; that's us!

In the excitement of the final chorus, Mr Darling collides with Nana on the
final chord and falls over her. He is immediately cross again. The children
roar with laughter which infuriates their father even more

Mr Darling That's it! That's the last straw! I've always said we shouldn't
have a dog for a nurse. She's covered me with hairs.

Mr Darling begins to brush himself down. Mrs Darling helps him. Nana takes
Michael over to his bed on her back

Mrs Darling George, Nana is a treasure.
Mr Darling No doubt, but I have an uneasy feeling at times that she looks
upon the children as puppies. It is about time that we reviewed the whole
situation.
Mrs Darling Oh no, dearest, I feel sure she knows they have souls ... and
without Nana there would be no-one to protect my children.
Mr Darling Protect ...? Protect? *(Proudly)* You have a husband, my dear,
to see his family is well provided for and comes to no harm!

Wendy and John disappear into the bathroom

Nana attends to Michael

Mrs Darling takes her husband aside

Mrs Darling I know, my love, but I am a little bit worried. I know it sounds
silly ... but I thought I saw a face at the window earlier this evening.

Mr Darling How could that possibly be? We're three floors up!

Mrs Darling Yes, I know, but it was the face of a little boy; he was trying to get in, George, and it is not the first time I have seen that boy.

Mr Darling Oh, no?

Mrs Darling (*making sure that Michael does not hear*) The first time was a week ago. It was Nana's night out and I had been drowsing here by the fire when suddenly I felt a draught, as if the window were open. I looked round and I saw that boy in the room.

Mr Darling In the room?

Mrs Darling I screamed. Just then Nana came back and she at once sprang at him. The boy leapt for the window. She pulled down the sash quickly, but it was too late to catch him.

Mr Darling I see ... Well, next time you should——

Mrs Darling Wait. The boy escaped, but his shadow had not time to get out; down came the window and cut it clean off.

Mr Darling (*heavily*) Mary, Mary. Why didn't you keep that shadow?

Mrs Darling I did. I rolled it up, George, and here it is.

She produces the shadow from the chest of drawers. It is made from flimsy dark netting material and is of human shape

Music 2A: Instrumental

Mr Darling Let me see that. Well it's nobody I know, but he does look a scoundrel.

Mrs Darling returns the shadow to the drawer

Mrs Darling Oh, George dear, do be serious. Recently, too, Wendy has been, well, telling me stories of a little boy called ... er ... Peter, who sometimes sits at the foot of her bed and plays music to her.

Mr Darling (*grinning*) And what music does he play!

Mrs Darling She says she's never awake. She just knows he's there.

Mr Darling Dreams, my love. You've always said our Wendy has a vivid imagination. Just dreams.

Mrs Darling sighs

Michael's raised voice is heard. Nana is trying to give him his medicine

Michael No, shan't! Won't! Will NOT! I WON'T have the horrible stuff. Take it away, Nana.

Wendy and John enter from the bathroom

Mrs Darling What is that, Nana? Ah, of course, Michael, it is your medicine.
Michael (*promptly*) Won't take it.
Mrs Darling Let's get him his chocolate, Nana.

Mrs Darling exits to get Michael a chocolate. Nana follows

Mr Darling (*calling after her*) Mother, don't pamper him. Come on, Michael, be a man. When I was your age I took my medicine without a murmur. I said, "Thank you, kind parents, for giving me bottles to make me well."
Wendy (*encouraging Michael*) That medicine you sometimes take, Father, is much nastier, isn't it?
Mr Darling (*bravely*) Ever so much nastier, and I would take it now as an example to you, Michael, if I hadn't lost the bottle.
Wendy (*helpfully*) It's not lost, Father. It's in the bathroom. I'll get it.

Wendy goes to the bathroom before Mr Darling can stop her

Mr Darling Wendy, don't!

John giggles

John, it's most beastly stuff. It's that nasty, sticky, sweet kind.
John (*grinning*) It will soon be over, Father.

Wendy rushes back with the medicine in a glass

Wendy I've been as quick as I could.
Mr Darling You have been wonderfully quick, precious quick!

Wendy hands the medicine to her father

Michael first.
Michael Father first.
Mr Darling I shall be sick, you know.
John Come on, Father.
Mr Darling Hold your tongue, John.
Wendy I thought you took it quite easily, Father, saying, "Thank you, kind parents ——"
Mr Darling That is not the point. The point is that there is more in my glass than in Michael's spoon. And it just isn't fair.
Michael (*coldly*) Father, I am waiting.
Mr Darling It's all very well to say you are waiting; so am I waiting.

Michael Father's a cowardly custard.
Mr Darling So are you a cowardly custard.
Michael I'm not frightened.
Mr Darling Neither am I frightened.
Michael Well then, take it.
Mr Darling Well then, you take it.
Wendy Why not both take it at the same time?
Mr Darling Certainly, are you ready Michael?
Wendy One, two, three, go!

Michael takes his medicine but Mr Darling slips his behind his back

John Father hasn't taken his!
Michael (*furiously*) Heh! That's not fair! (*He begins to sob*)
Wendy Oh, Father!
Mr Darling What do you mean by "Oh, Father"? Stop that row, Michael, I meant to take mine, but I — I missed it.

They all look at him doubtfully

Look here, all of you; I have just thought of a splendid joke. I shall pour my medicine into Nana's bowl and she will drink it, thinking it is milk! What fun!
Wendy No, Father, NO!

Mr Darling pays no attention

Mrs Darling enters, followed by Nana. She gives Michael a chocolate

Mr Darling Nana, there's a good dog. I have put a little milk into your bowl, Nana.

Nana wags her tail and rushes to her bowl R. She begins to lap at it, stops and looks reproachfully at Mr Darling. Her tail stops wagging and she creeps into her kennel

Mrs Darling (*smelling the bowl*) Oh, George, it's your medicine.

Wendy comforts Nana

Mr Darling It was only a joke. Much good my wearing myself to the bone trying to be funny in this house.
Wendy (*cuddling Nana*) Poor Nana, poor, poor Nana. Father, Nana is crying.

Mr Darling That's right! Cuddle her! Nobody cuddles me! Oh dear no! I am only the breadwinner. Why should I be cuddled, why, why, WHY!

Mrs Darling George, not so loud. The servants will hear you.

Mr Darling (*angrily*) Let them; bring in the whole world. But I refuse to allow that dog to lord it in my nursery for an hour longer. Out! Out! Out!

Children Father, no, please don't!

Mr Darling In vain, in vain. The proper place for dogs is the yard and there you go to be tied up this instant.

Mrs Darling George, George. Remember what I told you about the face at the window. Nana must stay to guard my children.

Mr Darling I have made up my mind and that is that! Am I master in this house or is this wretched animal? Come along.

He drags Nana out of her kennel and exits with her

The children climb into bed silently and Mrs Darling turns down the gas lamps. Nana's bark can be heard in the distance

John Listen to her; that is because he is chaining her up in the yard. She's awfully unhappy.

Wendy That is not Nana's unhappy bark; that is her bark when she smells danger.

Mrs Darling Danger! Are you sure, Wendy?

Wendy Oh yes.

Music 3: Instrumental

Suddenly and violently the window blows open

Wendy gives a cry

Mrs Darling turns, startled

John Is anything there?

Mrs Darling (*looking out of the window*) All quite quiet and still. Oh, how I wish I was not going out to dinner tonight. (*She closes the window*)

Michael (*sleepily*) Can anything harm us, Mother?

Mrs Darling No, my precious. (*She kisses her children in turn*) Good-night, my little ones.

Mrs Darling exits

There is a short pause, then Wendy slowly sits up

Wendy Michael ...? John?

There is no answer. They are both asleep

Wendy gets out of bed, goes over to the window and unfastens the catch. The orchestra plays the introduction to music 4

Music 4: Peter

Wendy (*speaking*)

	Peter, Peter,
(*Singing*)	Are you, are you there?
(*Speaking*)	Peter, Peter,
(*Singing*)	If so, tell me where.
	Peter, Peter,
	Is it, is it true?
	Peter, Peter.
	What I, what I know about you?

> *Chorus*
> You fly, fly through my dreams
> So high, high that it seems
> Your star is shining up there
> Wait for me, Peter.
> Peter, Peter,
> Someday you'll see
> I know you have to be free
> But think of how it would be
> If you took me.

> I've seen you, I've seen you
> When Mother comes saying "Good-night",
> You wait there at the window
> For her to turn down the light
> I've heard you, I've heard you
> When the leaves rustle I know
> You're out there but you're leaving
> So where, oh where do you go?

Repeat chorus

After her song Wendy goes back under the blankets and falls asleep

A small beam of light — Tinker Bell — dances through the window and the soft jingling of bells can be heard. The fairy dashes round the room and then disappears into a jug on the mantelpiece

Music 5: Instrumental

The windows open and Peter Pan flies into the room

Peter Tinker Bell. Tink, where are you? Oh, do come out of that jug and tell me, do you know where they put my shadow?

Tink comes out of the jug and jingles

Peter jumps at the chest of drawers and scatters the contents around looking for his shadow. He finds the shadow in one drawer

Music 5A: Instrumental

He shuts the drawer trapping Tink inside. He sits down and tries to put his shadow on but finds he cannot

Peter goes into the bathroom and returns with some soap

Peter tries to "soap" his shadow on. He cannot. He is cross and begins to cry. Wendy wakes up, sits up and looks at him.

Wendy Boy, why are you crying?

Peter gets up and makes a small bow which Wendy returns

Peter What's your name?
Wendy Wendy Moira Angela Darling.
Peter Mine's Peter Pan.
Wendy Is that all?
Peter Yes.
Wendy I'm so sorry.
Peter It doesn't matter.
Wendy Where do you live?
Peter Second star to the right and straight on till morning!
Wendy What a funny address!
Peter No, it isn't.
Wendy I mean, is that what they put on your letters?
Peter Don't get any letters.

Wendy But your mother gets letters?
Peter Don't have a mother.
Wendy Oh, Peter, no wonder you were crying.

Wendy gets out of bed and goes to him. *Peter backs away*

Peter I wasn't crying about mothers. I was crying because I can't get my shadow to stick on. Besides, I wasn't crying.
Wendy It has come off?
Peter Yes.
Wendy How awful! (*She picks up the soap*) And you've been trying to stick it on with soap. (*She stifles a giggle*) Peter, it must be sewn on.
Peter What's sewn?
Wendy You're dreadfully ignorant.
Peter No I'm not.
Wendy I shall sew it on for you. I dare say it will hurt a little.

She collects a needle, thimble and thread from her sewing basket on the chest of drawers

Peter Oh, I shan't cry, because I'm brave and OH!

Wendy sews on the shadow

The Lights change

Music 6: Instrumental

A large shadow is outlined against the wall. Peter dances with joy

Wendy Perhaps I should have ironed it.

Peter crows triumphantly

Peter!

Peter crows again

Peter (*crowing*) How clever I am! Oh, the cleverness of me! Wendy, look, look!
Wendy (*crossly*) Well, I ... of course, I did nothing.
Peter You did a little. (*He crows again*)
Wendy A little! Well if I am no use and all you can do is make that ridiculous noise I shall go back to bed. (*She springs into her bed and covers her face with the blanket*)

Peter Wendy, don't go away. I always crow when I'm pleased with myself.

Wendy does not move

Wendy ... Wendy, one girl is more use than twenty boys.

Wendy peeps over the bedclothes

Wendy Do you really think so, Peter?
Peter Yes, I do.
Wendy Well I think it's perfectly sweet of you and I'll get up again and I'll give you a kiss if you like.
Peter (*holding out his hand expectantly*) Thank you.
Wendy Surely you know what a kiss is?
Peter I shall know when you give it to me.

Wendy is about to kiss Peter when she thinks better of it and instead gives him the thimble she used in the sewing-on of his shadow

Peter (*looking at the thimble*) Now, shall I give you a kiss?
Wendy If you please.

Peter drops an acorn button into her hand

Oh ... I shall wear your kiss on a chain round my neck.
Peter (*shrugging*) As you please.
Wendy Peter, how old are you?
Peter (*uneasily*) I don't know, but I am quite young. Wendy, I ran away the day I was born.
Wendy What!
Peter It was because I heard Father and Mother talking about what I was to be when I became a man. (*He becomes agitated*) I don't want ever to be a man. I want always to be a little boy and to have fun. So I ran away to Kensington Gardens and lived a long time among the fairies.
Wendy But Peter, just think of all the wonderful things you'll miss: having a family, and a career, becoming rich and ——
Peter No, Wendy, listen ...

Music 7: What Happens (When You're Grown Up?)

(*Singing*)   What happens when you are grown up?
                     What happens when you are tall?
                     Shadows can no longer be sewn up
                     And your childhood things are too small.

       Wendy, I'm sure adult life is a bore
       Becoming thirteen is no joy
       So instead of school and then "studying law"
       I decided to stay as a boy.

Musical reprise of the first four lines during which ...

Wendy (*speaking*) But Peter, you can't just stay as a boy all your life. Just think how exciting it would be to be a man ... and a father. Peter, wouldn't you like to be ... married?

Peter (*singing*) Wendy, I'm sure adult life is a bore
       Becoming thirteen is no joy
       So instead of school and then "studying law"
       I decided to stay as a boy.

The song takes on an "up-tempo" and Peter struts about the stage

       I ran away from home the day that I was born
       And I went to Kensington Gardens.
       I don't care to wash my face, speaking when I'm spoken to
       For me there is no begging of pardons
       Wendy, you must understand
       Your parents' life is hard
       When they're dressed up fine and looking grand
       It's only a façade
       Too much responsibility
       Involved in being a man
       There's one little boy who won't grow up
       That's Peter Pan!

Musical reprise. Peter dances

       Wendy, you must understand
       A parent's life is hard
       When they're dressed up fine and looking grand
       It's only a façade
       Too much responsibility
       Involved in being a man

Peter   There's one little boy who won't grow up
Wendy   One little boy who can't grow up
Both   This one little boy will not grow up
       That's Peter Pan!

(*Speaking*) Talking of living with fairies, I wonder where Tinker Bell has gone to.

Wendy Peter! (*She clutches him*) Do you mean to tell me there is a fairy in
this room?
Peter Yes, she's my fairy. You know, there ought to be one fairy for every
boy and girl.
Wendy Ought to be? Isn't there?
Peter No, you see children know such a lot now, they soon don't believe in
fairies, and every time a child says, "I don't believe in fairies", there is a
fairy somewhere that falls down dead.
Wendy Oh how awful! ... but your fairy is here ... with you?
Peter Well, she was just now. You can't hear her, can you?

They both listen and Tink's muffled jingle can be heard

Wendy The only sound I hear is like a tinkle of bells.
Peter Well, that's Tink. That's the fairy language. I think I hear her too.
Wendy, I do believe I shut her up in the big box!
Wendy The big box? Oh, you mean the chest of drawers!

Peter opens a drawer. Tink flies out and about the room jingling madly

Peter Well, really, Tinker Bell, you shouldn't say such things.

Tink jingles

Of course I'm very sorry, but how could I know you were in there?

Tink jingles

And you're a silly ass too.
Wendy Oh, Peter, if only she would stand still and let me see her.
Peter They hardly ever stand still.

Tink disappears into the bathroom

Wendy (*sitting on her bed*) Peter, where do you live now?
Peter With the Lost Boys.
Wendy Who are they?
Peter They are the children who fall out of their prams when the nurse is
looking the other way. If they are not claimed within seven days they are
sent far away to Never Land. (*Proudly*) I'm their captain.
Wendy What fun it must be!
Peter Yes, but we are rather lonely. We haven't got a mother.
Wendy Are none of the other children girls?

Peter (*cunningly*) Oh no; girls, you know, are much too clever to fall out of
their prams.
Wendy I think it is perfectly lovely the way you talk about girls. You may
give me a kiss if you like.
Peter Yes, I thought you would want it back. (*He offers Wendy the thimble*)
Wendy Oh dear, I don't mean a kiss, I mean a thimble.
Peter What's that?
Wendy It's like this. (*She kisses Peter*)
Peter Funny! Now shall I give you a thimble?

Tink enters from the bathroom and dances over to Wendy

Before Peter can even draw near to Wendy, she screams

Peter What is it?
Wendy It was exactly as if someone were pulling my hair!
Peter That must have been Tink. I never knew her so naughty before.

Tink jingles

Wendy What does she say?
Peter She says she will do that every time I give you a thimble.
Wendy But why?
Peter Why, Tink?

Tink jingles

Peter She says, "You silly ass."
Wendy She is very impertinent and I shall therefore ignore her. Come, Peter,
let us sit over here.
Peter If you like.

They sit

Wendy Peter, why have you come to our nursery window so often? I've
always sort of known you've been there.
Peter To hear the stories your mother tells you. None of us know any stories.
Wendy How perfectly awful!
Peter Wendy, the other night your mother was telling you a lovely story.
Wendy Which story was it?
Peter About the Prince and he couldn't find the lady who wore the glass
slipper.
Wendy Peter! That was Cinderella and he found her and they lived happily
ever after.

Peter Hooray! (*He goes to the window*)
Wendy (*concerned*) Where are you going?
Peter To tell the lost boys.
Wendy Oh, don't go, Peter; I know lots of stories. Oh, just think of the stories
I could tell the boys!
Peter (*immediately excited*) Oh yes! Wendy, do come with me and tell the
other boys.
Wendy Oh dear, I can't. Think of Mother. Besides I can't fly.
Peter I'll teach you!
Wendy What!
Peter I'll teach you to fly.
Wendy (*clapping her hands*) Oh how lovely to fly!
Peter I'll teach you how to jump on the wind's back and then away we go!

The orchestra plays the introduction to music 8

Music 8: Come Away, Come Away!

	Chorus
(*Singing*)	Come away, come away
	To the Never Land.
	Oh, Wendy, let me teach you to fly
	Follow me, follow me
	To the Never Land
	Through the stars we'll soar up high
	It's not far, it's not far
	To the Never Land
	There are fairies and mermaids too
	Let's be off, let's be off
	To the Never Land
	Little Wendy, the lost boys need you.
	Just think what they'd say
	Seeing you coming their way
	I could tell them I'd brought them a mother
	Who would bid them good-night
	And tuck them up tight
	And tell stories one after the other

Repeat chorus

Wendy (*speaking*) Oh, Peter, you make it
Sound fascinating

(*Singing*)	But please say no more, not tonight,
	For I should not leave
	But I have this feeling
	In my heart that tells me I might ...
Peter	Come away, come away
	To the Never Land
Wendy	Would you really teach me to fly?
Peter	Follow me, follow me
	To the Never Land
	Through the stars, we'll soar up high!
Wendy ⎫	It's not far, it's not far
Peter ⎭	To the Never Land
Wendy	Oh I dreamed this would happen one day!
Wendy ⎫	Let's be off, let's be off
Peter ⎭	To the Never Land
Peter	Then you will?

Wendy nods excitedly

Wendy	I must ...
Wendy ⎫	Come away!
Peter ⎭	

Wendy Oh Peter? I'm so excited! Would you teach John and Michael to fly too?

Peter If you like.

Wendy runs to John's bed

Wendy John! John! Wake up! Oh do wake up! Peter Pan has come and he is going to teach us to fly!

John (*still half asleep*) What? (*Dreamily*) Oh, good.

Wendy John! John! Will you wake up!

Wendy turns the mattress, causing John to fall out of bed

Peter Pan is here and he is to teach us to fly.

John Is he? (*He sees Peter*) Why so he is! To fly, you say? Then I shall get up. (*He notices where he is*) Hallo, I am up!

Wendy by this time is shaking Michael awake

Wendy Michael, open your eyes. You are to learn how to fly. Peter Pan is here!

Michael (*sitting up in bed, rubbing his eyes*) Who?

John races round to Michael's bed and grabs him

John Come on, Michael.

Soon Wendy and John are talking excitedly to Peter, whilst Michael, still clutching his teddy bear, is endeavouring to understand what is going on. Then Nana's bark is heard off

Peter Quiet! Now stop blabbering and just listen! Hold on! I can hear someone coming. Quick, hide.

Sounds of Nana and Liza, a servant, can be heard off-stage

Liza (*off*) You silly dog, what do you mean by all this fuss?

Nana barks and growls off

> *The boys hide behind the curtains and in the bathroom. Wendy quickly puts the pillows under the bed covers in an attempt to show that all is well in the bedroom and that the children are sleeping peacefully. She hides*

Nana enters pulling Liza. They look around, all is quiet

There! You suspicious brute. They are perfectly safe, aren't they? Every one of the little angels sound asleep in bed. Listen to their gentle breathing.

Michael, encouraged by his success, snores loudly, nearly giving the game away. Nana is not fooled and barks, trying to pull away from Liza's grasp

Now that's enough! No more of it, Nana, I warn you if you bark again I shall go straight to master and missus and bring them home from the party, and then, oh, won't master whip you just.

Liza starts to pull Nana out of the room. Nana continues to howl as she is dragged across the stage

Stop it! Stop it, do you hear me? They must be stark raving mad having this animal as a nurse! Will you be quiet!

They exit and gradually their sounds die away

This Act has two alternative endings; the first, for performances for which harnesses and wires are not available, begins here

The children slowly come from their hiding places

John It's all right. They've gone. I say Peter, can you really fly?

Music 9A: Instrumental

Peter Simple. Watch! (*He flies — see Production Notes*)
John I say, how absolutely topping!
Michael Great!
Wendy Oh, Peter, how do you do it?
Peter You just think lovely thoughts and they lift you into the air, plus a little fairy dust of course.

Music 9B: Instrumental

Peter goes round each of them in turn blowing fairy dust on to them from his hand

Michael Ooh ... I feel all funny ... Wooaah!

Music 9C: Instrumental

Michael flies. His movements through the air are somewhat less graceful than Peter's earlier demonstration

   I ... I ... flewed!
John ⎤
          Hooray!
Wendy ⎦

The Orchestra begins to play the introduction to Music 10. The children practise their new-found flying powers again. There are shouts of joy from all

Wendy I'm flying ... I'm flying ... It's lovely. (*etc.*)
Michael Look at me! Weee! Whoops! (*etc.*)
John Oh, ripping good fun! What a wonderful way to travel! (*etc.*)
Peter Well, what are we waiting for? To the Never Land!
Wendy (*hesitantly*) Oh, Peter ...
Peter Mermaids!

Wendy Ooh! (*She can resist no longer*)
Peter And there are pirates!
John Pirates! Then let us go at once!

John grabs his top hat. Michael grabs his Teddy

Music 10: Come Away, Come Away! (Reprise)

All (*singing*)	Come away, come away
	To the Never Land
Children	Peter has taught us to fly.
Peter	Follow me, follow me
All	To the Never Land.
	Through the stars, we'll soar up high!
	It's not far, it's not far
	To the Never Land.
Peter (*speaking*)	There'll be danger, I give you fair warning.
All (*singing*)	Let's be off, let's be off
	To the Never Land
Peter	Second to the right
Wendy	Second to the right
John	Second to the right
Michael	Second to the right
All	And — straight — on — till — morning.

The windows open of their own accord. Peter beckons the children to follow him and as the number comes to its conclusion the children fly away to the Never Land

The Lights fade to a Black-out

CURTAIN

Music 11: Entr'acte

The following is the alternative ending to the scene for companies that are able to use wires and harnesses to "fly" the characters

John It's all right. They've gone. I say, Peter, can you really fly?
Peter Yes.

Music 9D: Instrumental

Peter flies dramatically

John Wow!
Michael Great!
Wendy Oh Peter, how do you do it?
Peter You just think lovely thoughts and they lift you into the air ... plus a
little fairy dust, of course.
Michael What's that?

*Peter moves to Michael, takes some fairy dust from his pouch and blows it
over Michael's head*

Music 9E: Instrumental

*Initially Michael shivers, then his eyes become wide and his mouth drops
open as the fairy dust magic begins to work*

Peter Now, Michael, concentrate. Think lovely thoughts — believe you can
fly and you will. Are you thinking?

*Michael screws up his eyes tightly as he endeavours to think of as many lovely
thoughts as he can*

Come on, Michael! Believe! Think! You can fly!
Michael I can ... yes, I can. I'm thinking ... I'm thinking.

*Slowly Michael rises from the ground; however, he still has his eyes shut.
Wendy and John watch Michael, gasping with delight*

Music 9F: Instrumental

Peter Michael, that's it! Go on, don't stop thinking. It will get easier and
easier.
Michael What? (*He looks down, realizes he is in mid-air, and screams. He
comes in to land*) I — I — flewed!

Wendy and John are anxious to learn how to fly

Wendy Oh, Peter, me too. Hurry!

Peter laughs and sprinkles fairy dust over Wendy

Peter Now Wendy ...

Wendy I know, think lovely thoughts. (*She closes her eyes tightly*) Um ...
sugar candy, walks in the park with Nana and ... and Mother's bedtime
stories! (*She flies quite gracefully*)

Music 9G: Instrumental

Oh! It's ... it's heavenly!

Peter (*moving to John*) Your turn, John. (*He sprinkles fairy dust over John*)

John (*clearing his throat importantly*) I say ... er ... I feel very peculiar. Now
then, let me see ... (*He closes his eyes*) A short career in the Grenadier
Guards, followed by running Father's firm! (*He flies and abruptly comes
in to land*) Well ... I say, how extraordinary!

*They all shout joyfully. Peter takes the opportunity to show off his very
considerable flying skills — until, finally ...*

Peter Well, what are we waiting for? To the Never Land!
Wendy (*hesitantly*) Oh, Peter ...
Peter There are mermaids ——
Wendy (*unable to resist any longer*) Mermaids!
Peter — and there are pirates!
John Pirates! Then let us go at once!

John grabs his top hat. Michael grabs his teddy

Music 10A: Come Away, Come Away! (Reprise)

All (*singing*)	Come away, come away
	To the Never Land
Children	Peter has taught us to fly.
Peter	Follow me, follow me
All	To the Never Land.
	Through the stars, we'll soar up high!
	It's not far, it's not far
	To the Never Land.
Peter (*speaking*) There'll be danger, I give you fair warning.	
All (*singing*)	Let's be off, let's be off
	To the Never Land
Peter	Second to the right
Wendy	Second to the right
John	Second to the right
Michael	Second to the right
All	And — straight — on — till — morning.

*The music swells with the key change and an instrumental version of the song
follows. Peter and the children fly*

*The scene changes, the Darling's nursery magically vanishing beneath them
so that soon they are flying high in the clouds through the night sky above
London, towards Neverland*

*Michael is just a little over-confident about this new-found mode of transport
and he begins to yo-yo around excitedly, generally bouncing along on the
clouds*

Michael Whee! Look at me! I'm flying! It's easy-peasy. (*He makes another
dramatic swoop*)
Peter Michael! Stop that! You'll tire yourself out too quickly. We will have
to keep flying until morning before we reach Neverland. And I don't intend
to carry you!
Michael (*suitably chastened, coming into line*) Sorry, Peter.

*And so the flight continues until morning. The music comes round for the final
time when the children, joined by a strong backstage chorus, sing:*

All	Come away, come away
	To the Never Land
	We're floating, we're flying, we're free!
Peter	Follow me, follow me
All	To the Never Land;
	A magical kingdom we'll see!
	It's not far, it's not far
	To the Never Land
Peter	Stay close, the new day is dawning ...
All	Let's be off, let's be off
	To the Never Land
Peter	Second to the right
Wendy	Second to the right
John	Second to the right
Michael	Second to the right
All	And — straight — on — till — morning!

*The number rises to a triumphant finish. Peter and the children fly away to
Never Land*

Black-out

Music 11: Entr'acte

ACT II
Scene 1

The Never Land. A clearing in the middle of a forest

The Forest is leafy and dense; the trees are old and have gnarled fairy-tale roots. There is a large tree trunk L, which has a hidden door. LC is a clump of red-spotted mushrooms, in the midst of which is a large prominent mushroom. It is big enough to comfortably act as a seat for a weary traveller

As the Lights come up, the Lost Boys are playing in the clearing. There are six altogether: Tootles, rather a simple sort of chap, the tallest and the leader in Peter's absence; Nibs, gay, happy and debonair; Slightly, rather conceited; Curly, who is a little timid with long tangled curly hair; and The Twins who are identical

Each Lost Boy is dressed in rough animal furs stitched inexpertly into patchwork patterns. They are all unkempt, unwashed and blissfully happy. All carry knives in their belts and Tootles and Nibs carry bows and arrows

Suddenly, in the distance, pirates can be heard singing and in a flash the Lost Boys, save Nibs, dive for cover through the door in the tree trunk with suitable cries: "Pirates", "Look out", " Hide — quickly" etc. Nibs disappears into the forest US, accidentally dropping his bow in his hurry

The pirates' singing becomes louder and closer

Music 12: Pirates' Song

Pirates (*singing; off*)
>Avast belay, yo ho, heave ho
>A-pirating we go
>And if we're parted by a shot
>We're sure to meet below!

The villainous pirates enter: Cecco, the Italian; Bill Jukes, tattooed all over; Gentleman Starkey, rather on the "wet" side; Skylights; Smee, an oddly genial man, old, eccentric, with spectacles; Noodler; Mullins

In the midst of them reclines James Hook, their captain. He lies at his ease in a rough chariot or sedan chair carried by his men. Instead of a hand he

*has an iron hook which he is polishing carefully. He is dressed in the attire
of Charles II and in his mouth he has a holder which enables him to smoke
two cigars at once. The pirates continue to sing*

> Yo ho, yo ho, the pirate life
> The flag o'skull and bones
> A merry hour, a hempen rope
> And hey for Davy Jones.

*Nibs briefly returns to retrieve his bow before retreating back into the
safety of the forest*

*But Starkey sights him. At once Starkey's pistol flashes out—but an iron claw
grips his shoulder*

Starkey Captain, let go.
Hook Put back that pistol first.
Starkey It was one of those boys you hate. I could have shot him dead.
Hook Ay and the sound would have brought Tiger Lily's redskins upon us.
Do you want to lose your scalp?
Smee (*brandishing his cutlass*) Shall I after him, Captain, and tickle him with
Johnny Corkscrew? Johnny's a silent fellow.
Hook Not now, Smee. He is only one and I want all six.
Smee All six! (*To the rest of the pirates*) The captain wants all six!
Pirates Ay — let's get all six.

General murmuring of agreement

Smee So — unrip your plan, Captain.
Hook The plan is simple; to return to the ship and cook a large rich cake of
a jolly thickness with green sugar on it. We will leave the cake on the shore
of Mermaids' Lagoon. The boys are always swimming about there trying
to catch the mermaids. They will find the cake and they will gobble it up
because, having no mother, they don't know how dangerous 'tis to eat rich
damp cake.

The Pirates laugh. Hook gives a particularly gruesome laugh

(*Pointedly*) They will die.
Smee And how d'you reckon to make such a cake, Captain?

The Introduction to Music 13 is played

Music 13: Rich, Damp Cake

Hook (*singing*) Take a tin with baking powder
                     Get some butter and some sugar
                     Collect fruit and nuts galore
                     A few ounces of flour
                     To give it extra power
                     With twenty-one eggs or more
                     Cream the margarine
                     Then add a little strychnine
                     A vital ingredient, make no mistake
                     My dear Smee, don't you see
                     We now have a recipe
                     For voluptuously dangerous
                     Rich damp cake!

                     Chorus I
All   Rich, damp; richy damp cake
Hook   Poor little Lost Boys easily led
All   Rich, damp; richy damp cake
Hook   One little bite and you'll find them dead.

Smee (*speaking*) Then what d'y'do, Cap'n?
Hook (*singing*) Then we'll put it in the oven
                     And wait till it has risen
                     And cover it with sugar that is green
                     And in case there's not enough
                     Of that lovely sickly stuff.
Smee (*speaking*) Add a little more strychnine?
Hook   Shut up!
                     And then to make it gleam
                     Smooth on the poisonous cream
                     And place it by the mermaids' lake
                     For they don't have a mother
                     A sister or a brother
                     To warn them not to eat my
                     Rich damp cake.

                     Chorus II
All   Rich, damp; richy damp cake
Hook   Fatal to boy, girl, mermaid or man

All	Rich, damp; richy damp cake
Hook	By Davy Jones we'll finish off Pan!

Then follows an instrumental verse and the pirates' dance routine. The pirates break upstage, singing harmoniously

> For they don't have a mother
> A sister or a brother
> To warn them not to eat my
> Rich damp cake.

Repeat Chorus I followed immediately by Chorus II

The song ends triumphantly

Hook Well, what are you standing around here for? Go to it, you swabs.

The pirates scatter and exit immediately leaving Smee and Hook alone

And most of all, Smee, I want their captain, Peter Pan. 'Twas he cut off my arm. (*He brandishes his hook*) I've waited long to shake his hand with this. Oh, I'll tear him.

Smee And yet I have often heard you say that one hook was worth a score of hands for combing the hair and other homely uses.

Hook (*ignoring Smee*) Peter flung my arm to a crocodile that happened to be passing by. Do you know that?

Smee I have often noticed your strange dread of crocodiles.

Hook Not of crocodiles—but of that one crocodile. It liked my arm so much, Smee, that it has followed me ever since from sea to sea and from land to land licking its lips for the rest of me.

Smee In a way, it's a sort of compliment.

Hook I want no such compliments! I want Peter Pan who first gave the brute its taste for me.

Hook sits on the large mushroom next to the tree trunk L

Smee, that crocodile would have had me before this, but by a lucky chance it swallowed a clock which goes tick tick inside it and so before it can reach me I hear the tick and bolt. (*He laughs*)

Smee Some day, the clock will run down and then he'll get you.

Hook (*his laughter cut short*) Ay, that's the fear that haunts me.

Smoke begins to rise from the top of the mushroom — and beneath Hook

Hook Smee, this seat is hot. (*He jumps up*) Odds bobs, hammer and tongs,
I'm burning!

The pirates return in confusion

Pirates What's up, Captain? (*etc.*)

They examine the mushroom by lifting its top. Smoke pours forth

Hook A chimney!
Smee We've found 'em, Captain. 'Tis clear those Lost Boys live here
beneath the ground.
Hook Now we have 'em, lads. The cake can wait ... When I give the order,
you ——

*A loud "ticking" is heard and we hear the first few bars of "The Crocodile's
Tune"*

Music 14: The Crocodile's Tune (Instrumental)

(*Shaking*) It's ... it's ... the crocodile! Get me away from here — hurry.

The pirates pick up Hook and in confusion carry him off stage

*The Crocodile slowly makes his way across the stage. As he exits the ticking
dies away and the Orchestra plays out the tune*

*Slowly the Lost Boys come up from the door in the tree trunk into the
clearing. Nibs, however, remains in the forest*

Tootles It's all right. They've gone.
Curly Phew! that was a near thing! I do wish Peter would come back.
Slightly I am the only one who is not afraid of the pirates — but you're right,
I'd like to see Peter again and he can tell us whether he has heard anything
more about the lady with the glass slipper.
Twins Yes, so would I.
Tootles My mother used to tell me stories like that.
Curly All I remember about my mother is that she often said to Father, "Oh,
how I wish I had a cheque-book of my own". I don't know what a cheque-
book is, but I should love to get one for my mother.

Nibs enters the clearing from the forest

Nibs (*out of breath*) Have you seen it? Have you seen it? It's a wonder, a wonder.

Slightly Seen what, Nibs?

Nibs The great white bird — it's flying this way.

Tootles What kind of bird?

Nibs I don't know but it looks so weary and as it flies, it moans "Poor Wendy".

Twins Poor Wendy!

Slightly I remember—there ARE birds called Wendies.

Curly (*pointing upwards*) See it comes. How white it is!

The Lost Boys look up and follow Wendy's progress through the clouds. Suddenly Tinker Bell's shrill voice can be heard

Slightly Look! There's Tinker Bell! Hallo, Tink!

Tink jingles

What!

Tink jingles again

Tootles She says Peter wants us to shoot the Wendy. Well, what are we waiting for? Let us do what Peter wishes. Quick — bows and arrows. (*He takes aim*) Out of the way, Tink. (*He shoots*)

Music 15: Instrumental

We hear a brief cry and Wendy appears, mid air. Slowly and limply, she drifts towards the ground, an arrow in her breast. She lands gently and the Lost Boys gather round her

I have shot the Wendy. Peter will be so pleased.

Slightly This is no bird. I think it must be a lady.

Tootles (*startled*) A lady?

Nibs And we have killed her.

Curly Now I see, Peter was bringing her to us.

Twin One A lady to take care of us at last and you have killed her.

Tootles I did it. When ladies used to come to me in dreams I said, "Pretty Mother, pretty Mother", but when at last she really came, I shot her. Friends, goodbye.

Peter crows off stage

Twin Two That's Peter.
Nibs Hide her!

Music 15A: Instrumental

Peter flies in and drops down in front of them

The Lost Boys stand in front of Wendy

Peter Greetings, boys.

They salute him in silence

(*Hotly*) I am back, why do you not cheer?

The silence continues

Great news, boys! I have brought at last a mother for you all.

Tootles drops to his knees

Have you not seen her? She flew this way.
Twin One Ah me!
Twin Two Oh, mournful day!
Tootles Peter, I will show her to you. Back everyone, let Peter see.

They all stand back revealing Wendy. Peter gasps

Peter (*kneeling beside Wendy*) She is ... dead. Wendy is dead. Perhaps she
is frightened at being dead. (*Sternly*) Whose arrow?
Tootles Mine, Peter.

Peter removes the arrow and makes as if to strike Tootles

Strike, Peter. Strike true.

*Twice Peter raises the arrow. Wendy raises her arm. Peter cannot stab
Tootles*

Peter I cannot strike. There is something stays my hand.
Nibs It is she! The Wendy lady; see, her arm.
Wendy (*whispering*) Poor Tootles.
Peter (*astonished*) She lives!

Peter kneels beside her and discovers his acorn button which Wendy had hung around her neck

Peter See, the arrow struck against this. It is the kiss I gave her. It has saved her life.
Slightly I remember kisses; let me see it. (*He looks*) Ay, that's a kiss.

Tink jingles

Curly Listen to Tink, she is crying because the Wendy lives.
Tootles It was she who told us you wanted the Wendy shot.
Peter What? Listen, Tinker Bell, I am your friend no more. Be gone from me forever.

Tink jingles

Well, not for ever, but for a whole ... week.
Curly Let us carry the Wendy down into the house.
Slightly Ay, that is what one does with ladies.
Peter No, no, you must not touch her. It would not be sufficiently respectful.
Slightly That is what I was thinking.
Tootles But if she lies there, she will die.
Slightly Ay, she will die; there is no way out.
Peter Yes, there is! Let us build a little house round her! Quick! Get to work.

Everybody obeys, building a house from forest materials

John and Michael fly in. They are exhausted

John Hallo, Peter.
Peter Hallo.
Michael Is Wendy asleep?
Peter Yes. Curly, see that those boys help in the building of the house.
Curly Ay, ay, sir.
John Build a house?
Curly For the Wendy.
John For Wendy? Why, she is only a girl.
Curly That is why we are her servants.
Michael You! Wendy's servants!
Peter Yes and you also. Away with them!

The brothers object but are very soon helping with the building of the house

Tootles If only we knew the kind of house she would like best.
Nibs Peter, she is moving!

Peter Wendy, tell us the kind of house you would like to have.

The introduction to Music 16 is played

                    Music 16: Wendy's Song (Part One)

Wendy   I wish I had a pretty house
                     The littlest ever seen
                     With funny little leafy walls
                     And roof of mossy green.

As they build the house, the boys echo Wendy's words

Boys   She wishes she had a pretty house
                     The littlest ever seen
                     With funny little leafy walls
                     And roof of mossy green.

Music interlude and Wendy's house takes shape

                     We've built the little walls and roof
                     And made a lovely door
                     So tell us, Mother Wendy
                     What are you wanting more?
Wendy   Oh, really next I think I'll have
                     Gay windows all about
                     With roses peeping in, you know,
                     And babies peeping out.
Boys   Oh, really next she thinks she'll have
                     Gay windows all about
                     With roses peeping in, you know.
                     And ... (*they look at each other, concerned*)
  (*Speaking*)   ... babies peeping out?

The flowers are collected and the house is decorated

Boys   We've made the roses peeping out
                     We're your babes for sure
                     We cannot make ourselves, you know,
                     'Cos we've been made before.

At the end of the song the boys stand back to look at their Wendy House

Peter There's no knocker at the door.

Tootles offers the sole of his shoe — it makes an excellent knocker

There is no chimney.
John (*importantly*) It certainly does need a chimney.

Peter snatches John's top hat, knocks out the bottom and puts the hat on the roof. The hat begins to smoke gently

Peter There! That's it! Now then everyone. All look your best; first impressions are awfully important.

Peter knocks politely. Slowly the door opens and Wendy steps out. The boys instantly either whip off their hats or bow

Wendy Where am I?
Slightly Wendy Lady, for you we built this house.
Nibs Oh, say you're pleased.
Wendy Lovely, darling house!
Twins And we are your children! (*They kneel*) Oh, Wendy Lady, be our mother.
Wendy Ought I? Of course it's frightfully fascinating, but you see I am only a little girl, I have no real experience.
Peter That doesn't matter.
Wendy Very well. I will do my best.

The boys cheer

Music 17: Wendy's Song (Part Two)

(*Singing*)   The first thing that a mother does
                     Is keep a tidy home
                     And to make sure that all her boys
                     Know how to use a comb

The boys look at each other, puzzled

John   Oh Wendy, they don't understand
                     So please explain some more
                     For comb's a word that I'm convinced
                     They've never heard before.

Music interlude. The boys line up and Wendy indicates that their hair needs tidying. The boys do so

Wendy (*sweetly*) The next thing boys it's plain to me
                  You don't know how to dress
                  For each and everyone I see
                  Is quite simply a mess.

The boys now look at each other, dismayed

Boys   We're sorry that we look a mess
                  There's one thing to make clear
                  With hand on heart we promise you
                  We changed our skins last year!

Music interlude. The boys now endeavour to tidy their and each other's attire

Wendy   I expect my children one and all
                  To mind their Ps and Qs
                  And no-one comes inside my house
                  Before they've cleaned their shoes

The boys look at each other uncertainly

Boys   Oh, Mother, we will try our best
                  But what's a P and Q?
                  And up till now we must confess
                  We've never cleaned a SHOE!

Music interlude as before. The boys line up outside the front of the house making vague attempts to smarten themselves up. Wendy marches along the line, inspecting the boys' hands and shoes. Peter looks on amused. At the end of the music interlude Wendy indicates the boys may now proceed into her house. They begin to do so and as they file in ...

Boys   You've made us tidy hair and clothes
                  There's nothing that you miss.
                  So, Wendy, what we want to know
Nibs (*solo, as he is the last boy to enter the house*) Are all mothers like this?

Peter, who is behind Nibs, quickly pushes him into the Wendy House before he has a chance to add to this last remark and, with a laugh, Peter himself disappears inside as the Lights fade to a Black-out

Music 18: Instrumental

SCENE 2

The Mermaids' lagoon. Early evening

Light effects and "dry ice" create the illusion of rippling water around the "Marooner's Rock," c

We discover Wendy and Peter playing on the rock. Wendy is peering curiously into the water

Wendy (*crossly*) Oh! Peter! You said if we came to the lagoon I would see a mermaid!

Peter I said you might see a mermaid, Wendy. Besides they are such cruel creatures that they would try to pull girls like you into the water and drown them.

Wendy How awful!

Peter Wendy, this is a very important rock. It is called Marooner's Rock. When a sailor has done something really dreadful the captain will bring him to this rock, tie him to this stake and leave him to be marooned.

Wendy Leave him on this little rock?

Peter (*unconcerned*) Yes. But they don't live long for when the tide is high the rock is covered with water and the sailor drowns.

We hear the loud laughter of Smee and Starkey in the distance and soon a dinghy containing the pirates and a captive Indian maiden — Tiger Lily — appears and makes its way towards the rock. Tiger Lily is bound hand and foot

Ho, ho! What have we here? Pirates! Hide yourself, Wendy, and we shall see what they are about.

Peter and Wendy hide from view as the boat reaches the rock

Smee Luff, you lubber. Here's the rock. Now then what we have to do is to hoist the redskin on to it and leave her here to drown.

Starkey This is your reward for prowling round the ship with a knife in your mouth.

Smee On to the rock with her, mate.

Starkey Not so rough, Smee; roughish, but not so rough.

They drag Tiger Lily on to the rock

Smee It is the captain's orders.

*Peter appears behind the pirates, unseen by them. Silently he motions to
Wendy to stay where she is and remain still. Seeing Tiger Lily's plight, he
"throws" his voice across the water, imitating Hook*

Peter (*imitating Hook*) Ahoy there, you lubbers.
Starkey The captain! He must be rowing out to us.
Smee (*calling out*) We are putting the redskin on the rock as you ordered,
  Captain.
Peter Set her free!
Smee Free!
Peter Yes, cut her bonds and let her go.
Starkey But Captain ——
Peter At once, d'ye hear, or I'll plunge my hook in you.
Smee This is odd!
Starkey Better do what the captain orders.
Smee Ay, ay. (*He cuts Tiger Lily's bonds*)

*Tiger Lily immediately slips into the water and joins Peter who waves to her
to disappear quickly*

*Hook enters from the other side of the lagoon in another dinghy, rowed by
a pirate, who then rows away*

Hook Boat ahoy! Ahoy there you lubbers.

Hook joins Starkey and Smee on the rock

Starkey Ah, there he is!

Hook sighs heavily

Smee He sighs.

Hook sighs

Starkey He sighs again.

Hook sighs

Smee And yet a third time he sighs.
Starkey What's up, Captain?
Hook The game's up! Those boys have found a mother.
Starkey Oh, evil day!
Smee What is a mother?

Wendy (*horrified*) He doesn't know!
Hook What was that?!
Starkey One of them mermaids.

Hook grunts

Smee Captain, could we not kidnap these boys' mother and make her our mother?

Hook considers the plan, then grins evilly

Hook Obesity and bunions! It is a princely scheme. We will seize the children and carry them to the boat; the boys we will make walk the plank and Wendy shall be our mother.

Wendy forgets herself again

Wendy Never!
Hook What was that?

Starkey and Smee raise their lanterns

Smee Nothing to be seen, Captain.
Hook (*looking*) Where is the redskin?
Smee That's all right, Captain. We let her go.
Hook Let her go!
Starkey 'Twas your own orders. You called over the water to us to let her go.
Hook (*thundering*) Brimstone and gall! What cozening is here! Lads—I gave no such order.
Smee It is odd indeed.

Peter crows and Hook looks about. (If possible, Peter hovers in mid-air, throwing his voice from various directions)

Hook Who are you stranger, speak!
Peter I am James Hook, captain of the Jolly Roger.
Hook (*hoarsely*) You are not; you are not.
Peter Brimstone and gall, say that again and I'll cast anchor in you.
Hook If you are Hook, come, tell me, who am I?
Peter A codfish! Only a codfish.
Hook A codfish!
Starkey A codfish?

Smee A codfish?
Hook A codfish?

Starkey and Smee draw away from Hook

Starkey Have we been captained all this time by a codfish?
Smee It is lowering to our pride.
Hook Wait just a minute.

The Introduction to Music 19 is played. During the song, Peter hovers, and flies above and slightly behind Hook. Hook remains puzzled as to why he is unable to see him

Music 19: I've Got A Funny Feeling

(*Singing*)	I've got a funny feeling
	There's more to this than meets the eye
	We're facing one small problem
	You say you're Hook, BUT SO DO I!
	Hook, have you another voice?
Peter	I have, so take your choice.
Hook	And another name?
Peter	Ay, ay, it's not the same.
Hook	Are you vegetable?
Peter	No.
Hook	Are you mineral?
Peter	No.
Hook	Are you animal?
Peter	No.
Hook	Are you man?
Peter	No.
Hook	Are you boy?
Peter	Yes.
Hook	Are you an ordinary boy?
Peter	Oh no.
Hook	Are you a wonderful boy?
Peter	Yes!
Hook	Are you in England?
Peter	No, I'm not in England.
Hook	Are you here?
Peter	Yes!

Hook (*wiping his damp brow, puzzled*) You ask him some questions, Smee.
Smee I can't think of a thing.
Peter Can't guess, can't guess. Do you give up?

Hook   Speak clear and straight if you can.
Peter   Very well then; (*speaking*) I am Peter Pan!

He lands dramatically in front of Hook

The orchestra plays a crashing chord

Hook What! Pan!

Music 20: Instrumental

(*Shouting*) Now we have him.

Starkey and Smee discover Wendy. Peter has drawn his sword and is fighting Hook who is lunging with the hook. Peter soon has the better of Hook and is about to plunge his sword into him

The music stops abruptly. Wendy cries out, alarmed as Smee has his cutless to her throat

(*Cowering*) Think boy! Think! And what about your precious new mother?

Peter reluctantly gives up his sword. Hook immediately jumps to his feet and wounds Peter in the shoulder. Peter cries in pain and collapses

(*Triumphantly*) And now we have them. The girl will go first and you, Peter Pan, will watch and then it will be my pleasure to terminate our acquaintance once and for all. Deal with it, Smee.
Starkey Deal with it, Smee.
Hook Slowly.
Starkey Slowly.

Smee feels the razor-sharp edge of his cutlass and is about to deal with Wendy when suddenly we hear the "tick tock" of the crocodile. Hook's manner immediately changes

Music 20A: Instrumental

Odds bobs, men, do you hear that! Get out of this place — protect me, save me — HELP!

Hook jumps into the boat moored to the rock, closely followed by Smee and Starkey who then row him off

The ticking dies away as the crocodile, we presume, follows the boat, off

Peter We are on the rock, Wendy, but it is growing smaller. Soon the water will be over it.
Wendy Then we must go.
Peter (*faintly*) Yes.
Wendy Shall we swim or fly, Peter?
Peter Do you think you could swim or fly as far as the island, Wendy, without my help?
Wendy You know I couldn't, Peter; I am just a beginner ...

Peter moans

What is it?
Peter I can't help you, Wendy. Hook wounded me. I can neither fly nor swim.
Wendy Do you mean we shall both be drowned?
Peter Look how the water is rising. We don't have much time.
Wendy (*frightened now*) Peter! Whatever shall we do? I ... I ... don't want to drown, Peter!
Peter There is no way off, Wendy. (*Resignedly*) Besides, to die will be an awfully big adventure.
Wendy (*desperately*) No!!

Music 20B: Instrumental

We can hear the sound of the waves as the tide begins to cover the rock. Wendy holds on to Peter, terrified, as ——

—— the CURTAIN *slowly falls*

Interval

SCENE 3

The Mermaids' Lagoon

Music 21: Instrumental

Peter and Wendy, barely visible now, are still holding on to each other. However, the "rock" has been replaced with a much smaller rock—so that the surrounding "dry ice" water gives the impression of a higher tide

Peter Be brave, Wendy. It will not be long now.

Music 21A: Instrumental

Just then the crocodile appears in the water and makes its way towards the rock. Its clock alarm goes off

(*Excitedly*) Wait a minute! The crocodile!
Wendy Oh! No!
Peter Wendy! He has come to rescue us. He knows that one day I shall deliver the rest of Captain James Hook to him — don't you, old chap?

The crocodile opens its mouth and burps loudly

Wendy Hooray! We are saved! What are we waiting for — let's go, Peter.

The two hang on to the crocodile and they all plunge into the water. "The Crocodile's Tune" plays as the Lights fade

SCENE 4

Music 21B: Instrumental

The Indian camp. The atmosphere is sombre and melancholy music can be heard

A totem pole stands in the centre around which the Indians are seated. Some of them are smoking pipes

Tiger Lily rushes into the camp. She is tired and her clothes are ragged

The music stops

Chief Tiger Lily, my daughter. (*He holds out his arms*)
Tiger Lily Father! (*She falls into the chief's arms*) The pirates ... they took me ... Smee ... Mermaid's Lagoon ... Marooner's Rock ... the tide ... ropes ... (*She breaks down and sobs violently*)
Chief But my daughter. You are free — from the pirates?
Tiger Lily Peter Pan rescue me. He imitate Hook's voice ... clever boy ... set Tiger Lily free.
Chief God of Sun, protect Pan! (*He raises his hands*) Himba Hoola Paiter Pun!

All the Indians raise their hands

Indians Himba Hoola Paiter Pun!

Tiger Lily No Father, you don't understand. I stay behind and listen — the pirates — they plot evil plan to kidnap Lost Boys and take new mother hostage — we must protect lost boys. They will all be killed ... pirates. (*She weeps hysterically*)

There follows a cry from all the Indians. They immediately prepare for their war dance

Music 22: Braves to War

The Indians dance round the totem. They should all possess musical bass or baritone voices

Chief   Paleface pirates threaten boys
                     Gather bows and scalping knives
                     Steal through forest, make no noise
                     Guard their home and save their lives.

                     Chorus
Indians   Braves to war, Braves to war
                     Leave behind Papoose and Squaw
                     Lost Boys safe; see to that
                     Tiger Lily free — make our pact.
                     Hum ... Hum ... Hum ... Hum ... (*etc.*)

Chief   Paleface pirates threaten boys
                     Indian time to do some stalking
                     Creep on Hook, make no noise
                     Plenty kill and tomahawking.

Indians repeat Chorus

Tiger Lily   Paleface pirates threaten boys
                     Need all braves that we can muster
                     Seek out Hook, make no noise
                     Deal with him like General Custer.

Indians repeat Chorus

Music 23: War Dance

The war dance continues. The Lights flash. The pace of the music quickens. The whole scene suddenly erupts and rises to a wild and noisy climax, culminating in a repeat of the chorus

Black-out

SCENE 5

The Lost Boys' underground hideout and the clearing above. The tree trunk can be seen clearly as the entrance to the underground hideout

Music 24: Instrumental

The Lost Boys, John and Michael are seated underground around Wendy who is just finishing a story

Wendy ... And so the prince married Snow White and everyone lived happily ever after.
Boys Hooray!
Wendy (*clapping her hands*) Right! Bedtime, my children.
Boys Oh no, Mother! One more story! Not bedtime yet.
Wendy No fuss now! Settle down all of you!

The Lost Boys, John and Michael groan but reluctantly agree to go to bed which means finding their various allotted spaces in the underground home and curling up on the floor

Wendy picks up a needle and thread and begins to sew

The Lights dim on the underground home and come up on the clearing in the forest above

The voices of Peter and the Braves are heard offstage

Peter (*off*) Hail, warriors!
Braves (*off*) Hail, Paiter Pun!

Peter and Tiger Lily enter the clearing

Peter The Great White Father is glad to see the Piccaninny warriors in forest protecting his wigwam from the pirates.
Tiger Lily Me Tiger Lily ... me his velly nice friend. Peter Pan once save me from the pirates many moons pass. Me no let pirates hurt him or boys. Braves have stayed in forest and will guard his home for many more moons away.

Peter It is good, Peter Pan has spoken.

Tiger Lily places her hands together and bows towards Peter several times as she walks backwards across the stage and exits

Peter makes his way towards the tree trunk, the entrance to the underground home

The Lights fade on the clearing and come up in the underground home

Wendy Children, I hear your father's step. He likes you to meet him at the door.

The Lost Boys, John and Michael bounce up and greet Peter as he enters the underground home

Boys Father! Father's home! Hooray!

Peter raises his hand and the shouting stops. He is tired

Peter I've told you! Don't call me that! Go to bed!

The Lost Boys exchange glances but they obediently return to their spaces

Peter frowns and sits

Wendy Peter. What is it?
Peter I was just thinking. It is only make-believe, isn't it, that I am their father?
Wendy (*primly*) Oh yes.
Peter You see, it would make me seem so old to be their real father.
Wendy But they are ours, Peter; yours and mine.
Peter But not really, Wendy?
Wendy Not if you don't wish it.
Peter I don't.
Wendy Peter ... what ... what are your exact feelings for me?

Peter considers

Peter Those of a devoted son, Wendy.
Wendy Oh, I thought so.

She sounds disappointed although she is not quite old enough to understand why. She goes and sits by herself at the extreme end of the underground home

Peter (*after a pause*) Wendy ... Wendy ... You're upset ... I don't think I
understand why ... but I'm sorry ... Wendy?

Wendy (*turning to him, almost desperately*) Oh Peter, are you sure you
wouldn't like to be a man?

Music 25 begins

Peter (*speaking; gently*) No, Wendy ... you don't understand, do you? I've
told you ...

Music 25 : Why?

Peter (*singing*)   How — can I explain? You still don't know me now.
Wendy (*speaking*)   Peter ... please, if only you'd ——
Peter (*singing*)   Where can I start? I just don't know how.
    (*Triumphantly*) Tell me a story, then we can pretend ——
Wendy (*interrupting; turning on him bitterly; singing*)
                No! You never stop to ask where will it end.
                So look at us now, did the dream disappear?
                We're two worlds apart, so why am I here?
Peter (*defensive; becoming angry*)
                Oh, open your eyes, come on, what do you see ... ?
                I can't be the person you want me to be!
    (*He is tired, and now becomes aggressive*) And why ... just tell me why,
                do you ask me to change for you?
                Why should you want me to?
                And when ... go on, tell me when you believed I'd grow
                up your way?
                And do I have no say
                About me?

*Wendy backs away. She has seen these stubborn and agitated emotions in
Peter before, but they have never been directed towards her. She becomes
nervous*

Peter (*realizing Wendy's discomfort; softly*)
                I wanted you here; I wanted to show you ——
Wendy   I loved the adventure, but it's wearing thin.
Peter   I wanted you near, I wanted to know you ——
Wendy   We played the game and no-one can win.
Peter ⎤ (*in harmony*) There was a time when it seemed you would be
Wendy ⎦   The change that I longed for, someone for me.

Peter	Don't say any more, it's all going wrong.
Wendy	If he'd listen, I know I could show him a way
Peter	Pretend just a little and you'll find you belong
Wendy	I don't want to hear you is all he can say
Peter ⎤ (*in harmony*)	To be talking like this, I can't understand
Wendy ⎦	And what will become of the story we planned?
Peter	So why ——
Wendy	Why?
Peter ⎤	Just tell me why
Wendy ⎦	
Peter	Should you ask me to change for you?
Wendy	Don't you see?
Peter	Why do you want me to?
Wendy	It's not for me
Peter	And why ... ?
Wendy	Why?
Peter ⎤	Go on, tell me why you / I believed I'd / you'd
Wendy ⎦	grow up your / my way?

And do I have no say ——

The music stops abruptly

— about me!

The orchestra finishes gently. Peter and Wendy look at each other, both realizing where each truly belongs — and it is not in the same place or time

Wendy turns, distressed, and goes and sits in a corner. John joins her

John Wendy, I think I remember our real mother but it is so long ago and she is so far away ... shall we ... shall we go home, Wendy?
Wendy Oh yes! Yes! Let us go home!

Tootles, who has overheard this, stands, dismayed

Tootles What! Not tonight! Not now!
Wendy At once! Perhaps our real mother is in mourning by this time. Peter, will you make the necessary arrangements?
Peter (*coolly*) If you wish it.

As the dialogue continues in the hideout Peter moves up into the clearing

Tiger Lily enters the clearing in the forest

The Lights come up on the clearing in the forest above. Peter is seen meeting Tiger Lily. He quickly instructs her in the return details

Boys (*protesting loudly*) No; we shan't let her go. Wendy, Wendy, stay. Chain her up! (*etc.*)

Wendy cries out

Wendy Tootles! I appeal to you.

There is silence

Tootles I — I am just Tootles, and nobody minds me. But the first who does not behave to Wendy like an English gentleman, I will blood him severely.

Tiger Lily signifies her understanding and exits into the forest

Peter returns to the hideout

The Lights fade on the clearing

Peter Wendy, I have asked the redskins to guide you through the wood as flying tires you so.
Wendy Thank you, Peter.
Peter Then, Tinker Bell will take you across the sea. Wake her Nibs.
Nibs You are to get up, Tink, and take Wendy on a journey.

Tink jingles

She says she won't.

Peter walks to the Fairy's chamber UC

Peter Tink, if you don't get up and dress at once, I will open the curtains and then we shall all see you in your négligé.

Tink jingles madly

That's better. I should hope so too.
Wendy (*addressing the boys in general but Peter in particular*) Dear ones, if you will all come with me, I feel almost sure I can get my father and mother to adopt you.
Nibs But won't they think us rather a handful?
Wendy Oh no, it will only mean having a few beds in the drawing-room and, if necessary, they can be hidden behind screens.

There are shouts of hooray and general agreement

Nibs Peter, can we go?
Peter (*with a bitter smile*) All right.

There are loud cheers

The Boys disappear US *in the hideout to fetch their belongings*

Wendy And now Peter, I am going to give you your medicine before you go.

Peter looks at her. She pours some liquid into half an empty coconut shell and puts it UC

Then you can get your things, Peter.
Peter No, I am not going with you, Wendy.
Wendy Yes, Peter.
Peter No !!!

Noisily and excitedly the boys return, ready for their journey. They carry knapsacks on sticks over their shoulders

Wendy Peter isn't coming.
John Peter isn't coming?
Tootles But why, Peter?
Peter Because I want always to be a little boy and have fun. If you find your mothers, I hope you will like them.

One of the twins starts to sniffle

Now then; no fuss, no blubbering. Goodbye, Wendy.

He holds out his hand. They shake hands solemnly

Wendy You will remember about changing your flannels?
Peter Yes.
Wendy And you will take the medicine I've left you?
Peter Yes ... Are you ready, Tinker Bell? Then lead the way!

At that moment there is an appalling noise above them off stage as the pirates attack the Indians

John It's the pirates!
Peter Get back, all of you!

Music 26: Fight Music (Instrumental)

The boys wait below listening to the cries, gurgles and screams coming from off stage

The Lights come up on the forest clearing

Tiger Lily rushes into the clearing. Her clothes are in rags and she is terrified. A pirate follows her. She tries to call out to Peter down the tree trunk but is stopped by the pirate who roughly puts his hand over her mouth and drags her off stage

An Indian enters into the clearing. He is chased by a pirate. Another pirate enters from the other direction and traps the Indian. The two pirates ensure the redskin's death. They drag the body away

The sounds of battle die and there is silence. Slowly from both sides of the stage, the pirates steal in, brandishing their weapons. They are the victors

Hook enters last and quietly makes his way to the tree trunk. He listens

Slightly The battle's over!
John Wait! We don't know who has won.
Peter If the redskins have won, they will beat the tom-tom; it is always their sign of victory.

Hook is delighted to have overheard this and signals to one of his men to fetch the tom-tom. This is done and the drum is passed to Hook who beats it with his hook

Peter (*listening*) The tom-tom. (*Gleefully*) An Indian victory!

Music 26B: Capture Music: Instrumental

There are loud cheers, then the Lost Boys, John and Michael make their way up the tree trunk one by one — only to be grabbed by the pirates who, quickly and silently, snatch each one before he can utter a sound. Wendy comes last and is met at the top by Hook who, with ironical politeness, raises his hat to her, and offering his arm, escorts her to the spot where the others are held. Wendy can do no more than gasp. She is too overwhelmed by the surprise of the situation to call out

The children are dragged off

The Lights dim in the forest clearing

Peter below is none the wiser

Peter, seeing all are gone, can now let out his bottled-up emotions. He weeps and is very soon asleep, exhausted and unhappy

Meanwhile Hook waits at the top expecting Peter to follow Wendy. When he does not, Hook silently makes his way down the tree trunk. He soon finds himself in the Lost Boys' home. He sees that Peter is asleep and creeps towards the medicine that Wendy left

Hook (*chuckling*) Well, well, well. What have we here? Medicine. That will serve my purpose.

Hook produces a small bottle from his pocket and is about to add the poison to Peter's medicine when the music starts and instead he begins to sing

Music 27: Goodbye Peter Pan

Hook   And so Peter Pan
                      To even the score
                      I'm here to bid you "Good-night"
                      Now your end has been planned
                      I'm not at all sure
                      That I want to finish the fight
                      It's a sad way to go
                      But you must understand
                      I couldn't continue to wait
                      And I'm sure you must know
                      When you cut off my hand
                      You finally sealed your fate ...

Hook again is about to poison Peter's medicine but instead continues

                      Goodbye, Peter Pan
                      My poison is strong
                      And you'll find there's no antidote,
                      Adieu, Peter Pan
                      It will not take too long
                      For the stuff to stick in your throat
                      Farewell, Peter Pan
                      Your demise will be quick
                      I'll make a fast-working brew
                      So long, Peter Pan
                      Just one simple lick
                      Will ensure the end of you.

The music builds — Hook continues more confidently and gleefully

                      Goodbye, Peter Pan
                      The battle is won
                      And it seems the victory's mine

Adieu, Peter Pan
The name "Hook" will live on
Whilst the memory of you will decline
Farewell, Peter Pan
You'll cease to exist
I find that's almost a shame
So long, Peter Pan
It's the ultimate twist
For we've come to the end of the game.

The music builds again. Hook is now wildly excited

Goodbye, Peter Pan
You've had your chips
Take your med'cine for "dear Wendy's" sake
Adieu, Peter Pan
When it passes your lips
You'll sleep and never awake
Farewell, Peter Pan
I'll miss you, you know
It's like saying "adios" to a friend
So long, Peter Pan
You gave a good show
But your story has come to the end.

Hook is again about to poison the medicine but, as though to draw out the triumphant final moment ...

Ta ta, Peter Pan!
Your number is up
It's true you put up a good fight
Adieu, Peter Pan
One sip from your cup
And you will go out like a light
Farewell, Peter Pan
When I think of the years
That I've waited for this, I could cry
I'll even admit I'll weep crocodile tears
To honour your past
To wish you at last
My dear, Peter Pan ...
Goodbye ...
GOODBYE!

Hook poisons the medicine. It froths dangerously and turns a different colour

Hook laughs loudly and evilly and exits up the tree trunk

Peter stirs. Soft jingling from Tink can be heard. It becomes louder. Peter wakes. Tink is jingling madly

Peter Tink?

Tink jingles and begins to chatter excitedly to Peter

Tink? Where are you? Oh, there you are ... What? ... Now steady, calm down. I don't understand WHAT you are saying. Pirates? Where? ... But I thought the Indians ... What! ... Hook has captured Wendy? ... And the boys! I must rescue them!

Peter is about to rush out when he remembers the medicine

Wait! — my medicine! Wendy would never forgive me.

Peter is about to drink the medicine when Tink jingles

Why not?

Tink jingles

Poisoned? Who could have poisoned it?

Tink jingles

Don't be silly. How could Hook have got down here? I think you are inventing all this because you didn't like Wendy leaving me my medicine. I do believe you're jealous. (*He raises the coconut shell to his lips*)

Tink jingles and drinks the medicine

Tinker Bell! How dare you! How dare you touch my medicine. Explain yourself!

There is no answer. After a pause

Tink?

There is a faint jingle and Peter is suddenly afraid

Tink! Tink! What ... what is the matter with you?

There is a faint jingle

Poisoned? Poisoned? Oh, Tink, you did it to save me.

There is a fainter jingle

Tink, Tink, don't die. Please Tink. Oh, Tink. Why, why? (*Addressing the audience*) Her light is growing faint. If it goes out, it means she is ... dead.

There is a very faint jingle

What? Believe? Believe in what? Tinker Bell? (*He begins to cry*) Of course I believe in fairies! Yes, yes ... the others believe in fairies, too, Tink — they must — they will — they do. Then you'll be well.

Tink jingles

Don't worry, Tink, we'll fight the poison — they believe, I know they do. (*In desperation he turns to the audience*)

Music 28: You've Gotta Believe

(*Singing through his tears*)
                I appeal to all the children
                To every one of you
                Say you believe in fairies
                It's the least that you can do
                I'm waiting for your answer
                A clap, a shout, a cry
                Don't let me down, everyone
                Don't let my Tinker Bell die ...
(*With great feeling*)

        Chorus
        You've gotta believe, you've gotta believe
        Oh, say you believe in fairies
        I'm sure you believe, I know you believe
        Tell me you believe in fairies.
        You've gotta believe, you've gotta believe
        Oh, say you believe in fairies
        I'm sure you believe, I know you believe
        Tell me you believe in fairies.

Peter buries his head in his hands as the music continues. He looks towards Tinker Bell whose light, by now, is very dim

(*Speaking through his tears*) Tink ... Tink ... please live ... you ... you must ... they all believe ... you'll see ... don't die ... Tink!

A recording " click-track" adds to the Orchestra as the instrumental verse comes to its end. Peter brushes the tears from his face. Then desperately but resolutely, he walks to the front of the stage, where he addresses the members of the audience

Everyone! Listen to me. Tinker Bell is dying. And all of you children here
are the only ones who can save her. And the only way you can save her is
if you tell her you BELIEVE IN FAIRIES. So I'm asking you now (*His
voice becomes choked as he cries out*) DO YOU BELIEVE FAIRIES?

*The Children in the audience are encouraged to shout back that "yes" they
do believe in fairies*

WHAT? Tinker Bell can't hear you? You're going to have to shout louder,
or she's going to die. Don't let her die! We can save her! COME ON!
AGAIN! DO YOU BELIEVE IN FAIRIES?

*The Children in the audience are encouraged to shout more loudly that they
do believe in fairies*

And all the grown-up children; do YOU believe in fairies?

*The adults in the audience are also encouraged to shout that "yes" they do
believe in fairies*

Tinkerbell's light begins to shine a little brighter, but she is still far from well

*The distant recorded sounds of clapping and children's voices shouting and
cheering are heard from the speakers at the front and back of the theatre. As
the music builds, the sounds of the recorded children also become louder*

(*More confidently*) If you believe in fairies, STAND UP! STAND UP
AND CLAP. (*He begins to clap above his head in time to the music as it
crescendos*) Yes! Yes! Clap! And stamp your feet. Mothers and Fathers
too. And all smaller children, climb on to your Fathers' shoulders where
Tinker Bell can see you. EVERYONE stand and clap and stamp your feet!
THAT'S RIGHT; COME ON! WE CAN SAVE HER!!

*The orchestra, the recorded "click-track" and the recorded children blend
with the furore of the audience stamping and clapping. Tinker Bell's light
slowly becomes brighter and brighter*

(*More excited; happier and happier and maybe weeping tears of joy*) It's
working! It's working! Don't stop clapping! Tink is getting better! Come
on, Tink! You can do it!

*Peter continues ad libbing, while a recording of children singing is heard
over the audience clapping*

Children (*singing, recording whilst the audience claps*)
      Yes, we believe, yes, we believe
      Oh we believe in fairies
      We're sure we believe, we know we believe
      Oh, yes we believe in fairies.

      Yes, we believe, yes, we believe
      Oh, we believe in fairies
      We're sure we believe, we know we believe
      Oh, yes we believe in fairies.

The music stops abruptly. But Peter encourages the audience to continue clapping loudly. The stage darkens enabling the audience to see clearly Tinker Bell's very faint light

Peter Tink?... Tink?...(*To the audience*) Come on! Don't stop now ... That's right! Louder! (*He encourages the clapping to grow*)

Tink jingles softly, then louder, and again louder. As she does so her light gradually brightens, until eventually the fairy is her old self again. Soon she is dancing happily over the stage

She's well! Tinker Bell is well again. We've done it! Oh, thank you, thank you!

Cheers from the audience and the recorded children are heard. The music starts again and the children (recorded) sing the chorus. By now, however, the audience should have grasped the tune and the words and, led by a happy and triumphant Peter, they are encouraged to join in the singing. The scene should now have developed into a lively and joyous celebration of Tinker Bell's recovery. Peter bounds off the stage into the auditorium. The auditorium becomes awash with flashing lights and colour. Peter meets and shakes hands with as many of the children in the audience as time will allow — until finally, at the song's happy end, Peter arrives back on stage c

And now Tinker Bell, are you ready?

Tink jingles sharply

Good! Then forward to rescue Wendy and the boys! To the *Jolly Roger*.

Music 29: Instrumental

The Lights fade to a Black-out

CURTAIN

ACT III

SCENE 1

The Pirate Ship

Music 30: Pirates' Song: Avast Belay

We discover Hook on board the pirate ship, prowling the deck. Smee is at his sewing machine mending a sail. The rest of the pirates, however, are not to be seen save two: one who is at the wheel on the upper deck and Starkey, who gazes dreamily out to sea. The "Avast Belay" chorus comes from the other pirates, off. It is early evening and the sun is beginning to set on the water

Hook (*as Barrie says, "communing with his ego"*) How still the night is; nothing sounds alive. Now is the hour when children in their homes are a-bed; their lips bright-browned with the good-night chocolate and their tongues drowsily searching for belated crumbs housed insecurely on their shining cheeks. Compare with them the children on this boat about to walk the plank. Split my infinitives, but 'tis my hour of triumph ...

Hook raises his leg to step on the side of the plank. Just as he does, Smee tears a piece of sail with a rending sound. Hook looks alarmed and checks the seam at the back of his trousers

... and yet some disky spirit compels me now to make my dying speech, lest when dying there may be no time for it. All mortals envy me, yet better perhaps for Hook to have had less ambition! O fame, fame, thou glittering bauble, what if the very ...

Smee, engrossed in his labours, at the sewing machine, tears another piece of sail which once more makes Hook think for a moment that the untoward has happened to his trousers. He cautiously examines himself

No little children love me. I am told they play at Peter Pan, and that the strongest always chooses to be Peter. They would rather be a twin than Hook; they force the baby to be Hook. The baby! That is where the canker gnaws.

Smee burps loudly. Hook studies him

'Tis said they find Smee lovable. But an hour agone I found him letting the youngest of them try on his spectacles. Pathetic Smee, the nonconformist pirate, a happy smile upon his face because he thinks they fear him! How can I break it to him that they think him lovable? No, bi ... carbonate of soda, no, not even ...

Another rending of the sail disturbs him, and he has a private consultation with Starkey, who turns him round and evidently assures him that all is well

Eight bells strike

Music 31: Instrumental

The remainder of the pirates pour forth from various parts of the ship, loudly and raucously

Quiet, you dogs, or I'll cast anchor in you! Are all the children chained, so they cannot fly away?
Pirate Ay, ay.
Hook Then hoist them up.
Starkey Tumble up, you ungentlemanly lubbers.

The prisoners, except Wendy, are dragged from the hold. They are arranged in a line in front of Hook

Hook Now then, you bullies, six of you walk the plank tonight, but I have room for two cabin boys. Which of you is it to be?

Nobody steps forward. Then, during the course of the next exchanges between the Lost Boys, Hook makes his way down the line waiting for each boy's decision

Tootles You see, sir, I don't think my mother would like me to be a pirate. Slightly, would your mother like you to be a pirate?
Slightly I don't think so. Nibs, would your mother like you to be a pirate?
Nibs I don't think so. Curly, would your mother like you to be a pirate?
Curly I don't think so. Twins, would your mother like you to be a pirate?
Twins (*together*) I don't think so. John, would your mother like you to be a pirate?
John (*to Michael*) I don't think so. Michael, would your mother like you to be a pirate?

Hook arrives at Michael

Michael (*to Hook*) I don't think so. Hook, would your mother like you to be a pirate?

Hook (*confused*) Well, no, I don't think so ... aaargh!!! (*Roaring*) Stow this gab! Bring up their mother.

Wendy is brought from the hold

(*Syrupy*) So my beauty — you are to see your children walk the plank!
Wendy Are they to die?
Hook They are!

The pirates snigger

Silence all! ... for a mother's last words to her children.
Wendy (*grandly*) These are my last words, dear boys. I feel that I have a message to you from your real mothers and it is this: we hope our sons will die like English gentlemen.
Hook Tie her up!

Smee ties Wendy up

Let her watch her children go!
Smee (*whispering to Wendy*) See, here, honey: I'll save you if you promise to be my mother.
Wendy I would almost rather have no children at all.
Hook (*turning to the boys*) Right, you swabs — who is to be the first?

Music 31A: Instrumental

Just then the "tick tock" sound of the Crocodile is heard. An immediate change comes over Hook. He listens and begins to shake

(*Hoarsely*) Hide me!

The pirates gather round him — all faces turned inwards

Peter flies on to the boat, carrying a large alarm clock. He signals everyone to keep quiet and disappears into the hold unseen by the pirates

The pirates disperse and Hook is discovered cowering. Slowly he becomes himself again

Music 32: Pirates' Song (Reprise)

Hook   Then here's to Johnny Plank!
                            Yo ho, yo ho, the frisky plank,
                            You walk along it so,
                            Till it goes down, and you goes down
                            To Davy Jones below!

The boys counter Hook by singing "Rule Britannia"

(*Speaking angrily*) Do you want a touch of the cat before you walk the plank?
Boys (*feigning fear*) No, no. (*etc.*)

Some of the boys go down on their knees

Hook Fetch the cat, Jukes, it's in the cabin.
Jukes Ay, ay, sir.

He enters the hold

Hook begins to sing again

Hook   Yo ho, yo ho, the scratching cat
                          Its tails are nine, you know
                          And when they're writ upon your back ...

There is a terrible scream from Jukes inside the hold. Peter has obviously "dealt" with him. Peter follows the scream by crowing

Slightly (*solemnly*) One!
Hook What was that?

Cecco puts his head inside the hold

What's the matter with Bill Jukes, you dog?
Cecco The matter wi' him is he's dead ... stabbed!
Pirates (*general concern*) What! Bill Jukes dead! (*etc.*)
Cecco The cabin's as black as a pit — but there is something terrible in there: the thing you heard crowing.
Hook Cecco—go back and fetch me out that doodle-doo.
Cecco (*cowering*) No, Captain, no. (*Panic-stricken, he starts gibbering in Italian*) La mia madre sempre midisse, "Non parla con stranieri". Ah, Mamma mia! ...
Hook (*cleaning his hook and holding it above Cecco*) Did you say you would go, Cecco?

Slowly Cecco enters the hold. They all listen. After a pause another terrible death-screech is heard followed by a crow

Slightly Two!
Hook S'death and oddsfish! Who is to bring me that doodle-doo?
Starkey Wait till Cecco comes out.
Hook I think I heard you volunteer, Starkey.

Starkey No, by thunder. I'll swing before I go in there. Mercy, Captain, mercy!

Hook (*lifting his claw*) Shake hands, Starkey.

Desperately Starkey looks round for support — there is none. He trembles, draws his sword and slowly walks towards the hold. Just before he enters, he turns, but Hook is right behind him

Starkey disappears. There is an even more blood-curdling scream — and Peter's crow

Slightly (*after a pause*) Three!

Hook seizes a lantern

Hook By Davy Jones, I'll bring out that doodle-doo myself.

Hook enters the hold — only to come out again very quickly. His lantern has gone out. He is shaking with fright

(*Unsteadily*) Something blew out the light.

Pirate What of Cecco?

Pirate And Starkey?

Hook They're both as dead as Jukes!

Pirates (*dismayed*) The ship's doomed! Aahh!

Hook Lads! Here's a notion. Open the door of the hold and drive the prisoners in. Let them fight the doodle-doo for their lives. If they kill him, we're so much the better; if he kills them we're none the worse.

The boys are driven into the hold

The pirates stare at the door of the hold and don't notice as:

Peter comes round the back and frees Wendy

Wendy quietly disappears down the other end of the ship while Peter takes her cloak and, covering himself, takes up her former position. He then crows. There is immediate panic among the pirates

Hook Lads, I've thought it out. There's a Jonah aboard — the girl! Never was luck on a pirate ship with a woman on board. We'll right the ship when she's gone. (*He turns to the cloaked figure*) There's none can save you now, Missy!

Peter (*from behind the cloak*) There's one!

Hook Who's that?

Peter (*throwing back the cloak*) Peter Pan, the avenger! Down boys and at them.

Music 33: Fight Music (Instrumental)

The Lost Boys emerge from the hold, armed to the teeth. There is a battle. The pirates are completely taken by surprise. One by one they are defeated and either jump or are thrown overboard

Hook and Peter face each other. The rest stop and form a ring around them

Put up your swords, boys. This man is mine.

Hook So, Pan, this is all your doing.

Peter Ay, James Hook. It is all my doing.

Hook Proud and insolent youth. Prepare to meet thy doom!

Peter Dark and sinister man, have at thee!

The sword fight begins. The Captain also makes frighteningly threatening use of his hook. After a few moments Peter cunningly flips Hook's sword from his hand and has him at his mercy

Pick up thy sword, James Hook — no more chances!

They fight again. Eventually Peter drives Hook right to the edge of the plank. The ticking begins below him. Hook is terrified. He begins to howl like a baby. Peter raises his sword, Hook cowers, loses his balance and, with a terrible scream, falls overboard. There is a noisy splash, a pause and a very loud burp from the Crocodile. Captain Hook's hook is spat out by the Croc. It lands on the deck at Peter's feet. He picks it up and holds his trophy high

Slightly Ten!

Wendy appears

Peter meets Wendy and takes her hand. They look into each other's eyes. There is a cheer from the boys

Music 34: Fanfare (Instrumental)

The Lights fade to a Black-out

SCENE 2

Somewhere in the Never Land — front cloth

Music 35: We're Going Home

John, Michael, Wendy and the Lost Boys march in confidently and joyfully — Peter is nowhere to be seen

Boys   We're going home and that's a fact
                  We're growing-up, we're going back
                  To be part of society, not this unruly mob

	We'll go to university and then we'll get a job.
	We'll fly away from our old life
Nibs	We'll fall in love
Slightly	We'll find a wife
Boys	And when we join the world of men
	Who knows what we may find?
	The Lost Boys won't be lost again
	It's time to leave the make-believe behind!
	We're going home, we're on our way
	We've thought it through, no need to stay
Twins	We're fond of doing nothing, to work would be a shame
Wendy	There are men like that in England, Civil Servants is their name
Boys	We'll fly away, we've made our plans
Tootles	To new horizons
Curly	Explore new lands
Boys	As upright citizens for sure
	Considerate and kind
	The Lost Boys won't be lost no more
	It's time to leave the make-believe behind!
	We're going home, we'll find out how
	To be grown-up, we're starting now
Tootles ⎤	What job for us two brainless chaps?
Curly ⎦	If you get our gist
Wendy	You're good at talking nonsense, become a journalist.

Tootles and Curly cheer

Boys	We'll fly away into the night
Twin One	We'll disappear
Twin Two	Far out of sight
Boys	To foreign places we are bound
	We've made up our mind
	Now the Lost Boys have been found
	It's time to leave the make-believe behind!
	We're going home, the battle's won
	And our new story has just begun
Slightly ⎤	And yet we have no special skill
Nibs ⎦	Whatever can we be?
Wendy	You're very self-important — you'll make a fine MP.

Slightly and Nibs cheer. Then look at each other uncertainly

Boys   We'll fly away, to re-arrange
                            Our lives so far, time for a change
                            Very soon now we have planned
                            Additions to mankind
                            We're going to quit the Never Land
                            It's time to leave the make-believe behind!

*At the end of the number, the Lost Boys, John and Michael charge off,
cheering*

Wendy goes to follow but then stops and turns

Music link ...

Music 36: Peter (Reprise)

Wendy (*speaking*) Peter ... I know you're here, somewhere ... listening. Oh
Peter!
    (*Singing*)   You fly, fly through my dreams
                            So high, high that it seems
                            Your star is shining up there
                            Stay with me, Peter
                            Peter ... Peter
                            Come, come and see
                            New home, a new family
                            Just think of how it would be
                            Please come with me.

*Wendy gazes front as though waiting for Peter finally to change his mind and
join them on the journey home. But he does not appear*

*John enters and sees Wendy's dilemma as to whether she should leave
without Peter*

John (*softly*) Wendy? Wendy, we're all ready to go. We must fly now the
wind is down.
Wendy (*resignedly*) Yes. I know.

Wendy looks back once more, then runs off with John

Come on!

Wendy and John exit

At that moment, Peter and Tink enter from the other direction

Peter They have all gone, Tinker Bell. They have left us alone. (*He thinks and then smiles ruefully*) But not for long! I have a plan. Quick, Tink! We will race them there and bar the window so they cannot get in. Hurry!

Tink jingles and follows Peter out

Black-out

SCENE 3

The children's bedroom

Music 36A: Instrumental

Mrs Darling is gently rocking in a rocking chair with her back to the window. Nana dutifully is laying out the children's night-time attire as she has done ever since they left

Mrs Darling (*waking with a start*) Wendy! John! Michael!

Nana goes over to Mrs Darling and puts her paw on her lap

Oh, Nana, I dreamt my dear ones had come back. I see you have put their night things out again, Nana. It touches my heart to watch you do that night after night. But they will never come back.

Liza enters

Liza Nana's dinner is served.

Nana bounds out

To think I have a master that has changed places with a dog!

Liza exits

Mrs Darling sighs and closes her eyes again. She is about to nod off to sleep once more

Mr Darling enters. He is dressed in a city pin-stripe suit, wearing a bowler hat and carrying an umbrella. He hangs up his hat and umbrella, walks over to Nana's kennel and begins to enter it feet first

Mr Darling Evening, dear.

Mrs Darling Good-evening, my dearest ... a good day at the office?

Mr Darling I'm just dead. Ah, dear!

Mrs Darling Oh George, you are as full of remorse as ever, aren't you?

Mr Darling See my punishment! Living in a kennel! My love, do shut that window, I feel a draught.

Mrs Darling No, George, no. Never ask me to do that. The window must always be left open for them just in case one day they — they ...

Mr Darling I know, my love, that was thoughtless of me. Of course we must leave the window open ... always.

Mrs Darling again falls asleep in her chair

Mr Darling snuggles into Nana's kennel

The stage darkens

Music 36B: Instrumental

Ideally Peter Pan flies into the room. If this is impractical, he simply enters through the window. Tink follows. Peter looks about him

Peter Quick, Tink. Close the window; bar it. That's right.

The window closes as if Tink has closed it

Now you and I must get away by the door, and when Wendy comes she will think her mother has barred her out and she will have to come back with me ... (*He notices Mrs Darling asleep in the rocking chair. He looks at her curiously*) Tink, this is Wendy's mother. She is a pretty lady, but she — she is crying ... I — I think she wants us to unbar the window but I won't! Not I! She's — she's awfully fond of Wendy. But I'm fond of her too and we can't both have her, lady.

There is a pause. Peter makes as if to leave through the door when Mrs Darling holds out her arm and in her sleep calls to him

Mrs Darling Oh Peter ... Peter ... bring them back to me. Bring my little ones back home. Wendy, John and Michael. (*She tosses and turns, dreaming*) Oh Peter, Peter ... don't let my children stay away too long.

Peter (*turning*) But — but Wendy belongs to me, lady. (*His voice begins to shake with uncertainty*) Wendy is to stay with me and be my mother. (*He becomes more confident*) You will never see Wendy again, lady, for the window is closed.

Mrs Darling Wendy, John, Michael ... Oh Peter, bring them back to me ... one day.

Peter stares at Mrs Darling, reluctantly realizing where Wendy and the others truly belong. He becomes angry and upset

Peter Oh, all right.

The window opens

We don't want any silly mothers anyway, do we, Tink? Come on!

Music 37: Instrumental

Peter and Tinker Bell fly off into the night

The stage brightens gradually as the orchestra begins to play and soon Wendy, John and Michael appear at the window and cautiously enter the nursery. They look around

Michael John, I think I've been here before.
John Of course you have, silly. Look, there is your old bed. I say! The kennel!
Wendy Perhaps Nana is inside it.
John (*looking in*) Hallo, there's a man inside it.
Wendy (*looking in*) It's Father.
Michael Let me see Father. (*He looks*) He is not as big as the pirate I killed
— and who's that? (*He points to Mrs Darling*)
Wendy Why! That's Mother!
Michael Then you are not our real mother, Wendy?
Wendy Oh dear! It's quite time we came back.
John Let us creep up behind her and put our hands over her eyes.
Wendy No, let us all slip into our beds and be there when she wakes up, just as if we had never been away.

The children all agree and do just that

Music 38: Instrumental

Wendy (*calling*) Mother!
Mrs Darling (*answering in her sleep*) That's Wendy.
John (*calling*) Mother!
Mrs Darling That's John.
Michael (*still rather uncertainly*) Mother?
Mrs Darling And, oh, that's Michael, and when they call I stretch out my arms to them, but they never come, they never come.

Mrs Darling stretches out her arms — only to find this time that her three children are in them. She wakes and can't believe her eyes

Oh, George, George!

Mr Darling wakes from his sleep, comes out of Nana's kennel and shares the excitement

Nana enters and barks

It is a joyous scene

Then, in the midst of the jubilation, faces begin to appear at the nursery window; first one and soon several

Wendy Come in, boys!

Almost sheepishly, the Lost Boys climb through the nursery window one by one

Mrs Darling Wendy! Whoever ...?
Wendy Mother, these are the boys from the Never Land. This is Nibs, Tootles, The Twins, Curly and Slightly. They have returned with us and we are to adopt them.
Mr Darling (*counting the boys; groaning*) Ohh no!! (*He goes over to one of the beds and puts his head in his hands*)

Nana joins Mr Darling beside the bed and puts her head in her paws

Nana (*a dog groan*) Ohh, no!!
Wendy Boys, this is my mother.
Mrs Darling Wendy, we can't possibly ...
Slightly (*taking Mrs Darling's hand and kissing it gallantly*) Wow! Now she is a beauty!
Twins (*dreamily*) At last, a real mother to take care of us.

The Lost Boys all look imploringly at Mrs Darling who looks from them to her husband

Mrs Darling George?

Mr Darling shrugs heavily and resignedly

Mr Darling (*muttering barely audible to the audience*) Brimstone and gall!

Nana barks. Mr Darling barks back. Nana sprawls flat on her tummy

Wendy Mother ...? Please ...?

Mrs Darling laughs and holds out her arms

Mrs Darling Very well.

Enormous cheering. Mrs Darling hugs the Lost Boys

Liza enters and joins in the celebration

Music 39: The Darlings (Reprise)

Wendy **John** **Michael**	We came back; I bet you thought you'd lost us
Wendy	I can't describe the adventures that we've had
John	We actually flew
Michael	I killed a pirate or two
Wendy **John** **Michael**	But we're home, of that we're very glad
Wendy	Oh, Mother don't be angry with Peter He saved my life, there can be no doubt
Wendy **John** **Michael**	Sorry we went away But now we're home to stay And once again we all can stand and shout ...

Nana howls joyfully to the music

All	Oh we are the Darlings Everyone a Darling It's the title of our family And it's hard to ascertain Quite where we got the name
Lost Boys	I'm just a Darling! That's me
All	Yes, we are the Darlings Remember we're the Darlings But there's no cause to make a fuss For as people walk our way We are very proud to say We're the Darlings, that's us!

They all exit, except Wendy and Mrs Darling, laughing and talking. Their voices die away but the music continues

Mrs Darling turns to find Wendy sitting by herself

Mrs Darling (*softly*) Your thoughts are still there with him, aren't they? Wendy, why did Peter not come back with the others? We would have looked after him.

Wendy (*loyally—for she has heard it a hundred times before*) No, he wants always to be a little boy and have fun. Besides, you wouldn't be able to see him very well. You can't see Peter clearly if you are grown up. Mother, I wanted so much ... I wanted ...

Mrs Darling holds her miserable Wendy close. She understands

Mrs Darling Why don't you visit him?

The idea had not occurred to Wendy. She looks up sadly

Wendy Visit him?

Mrs Darling Yes, next year—and every year! I don't suppose he has anyone to spring clean for him.

Wendy smiles, happier now. She nods and dries her eyes. Mrs Darling kisses her gently on the forehead

We will be downstairs. There are a lot of extra hungry mouths to feed. Don't be too long.

Mrs Darling leaves the nursery

Peter Pan flies into the nursery. He has been crying and has a tear-stained face

He looks around as Wendy stands alone, smiling; she starts

Wendy Peter!

Peter (*embarrassed*) Er ... hallo, Wendy. I just came to say. That is ...

Wendy Yes, Peter?

Peter I should like ... to give you back your thimble.

Wendy holds out her hand, expecting to receive the thimble she gave Peter when they first met

Wendy Very well.

Music 40: Don't Say Goodbye

Slowly Peter kisses her on the cheek. Wendy stands with her mouth open not knowing quite what to say. She is thrilled. Peter slowly backs away towards the window. He drops his eyes to the ground and turns to go

Peter ...

Peter turns back

Wendy If you like, Mother says I can come and spring clean for you once a year.
Peter (*his face brightening*) Oh, yes. Wendy! Yes!
Wendy Then I shall. I promise.

Peter heads for the window, crowing

Peter (*turning, smiling*) See you next year, Wendy.
Wendy (*stifling a sob*) Yes. Goodbye, Peter.
Peter (*holding out his hand suddenly*) No! (*He moves towards Wendy; singing*)

> Don't say goodbye, it's not the end
> I'm never far away
> So close your eyes and dream
> And I will seem to be
> Here by your side and I will mend
> The hurt you feel today
> Don't say goodbye, just try
> To understand I'm me.
>
> Don't cry too much when I am gone
> Or talk about my name
> There comes a time that we all know
> Where we belong
> Don't think of when we meet again
> If it will be the same
> Don't cry too much, just smile
> Be happy now, be strong
>
> And when you're lonely, remember
> What I say
> For though I'm leaving, don't stop believing,

That I am thinking of you
While I am away

Don't try to lose what we had found
Believe in what we knew
Don't wonder how we came to now
Don't wonder why
Don't ask me to forget you too
Don't throw away what we've been through
Don't say goodbye
Don't say goodbye

Peter flies away through the window as he sings the following

Don't say goodbye.

His voice dies away into the distance. The music from the orchestra swells

Wendy rushes to the window, waving. The music arrives at its tumultuous climax and ——

—— the CURTAIN *falls*

Music 41: Curtain Call: Instrumental

Music 42: You Gotta Believe (Reprise)

And if desired a full company version of Music 40: Don't Say Goodbye, *led by Peter Pan*

FURNITURE AND PROPERTY LIST

ACT I

On stage: Gas lamps
Three beds
Chest of drawers. *On it*: Top hat, sewing basket containing needle, thread, thimble. *In a drawer*: shadow
Mantelpiece. *On it*: jug
Beside table. *On it*: medicine in a glass, teddy
Dog's bowl
Dog's kennel
Dressing as desired

Off stage: Medicine in a glass (**Wendy**)
A chocolate (**Mrs Darling**)
Bar of soap (**Peter Pan**)

Personal: **Mr Darling**: white bow tie
Peter Pan: acorn button, fairy dust

ACT II

Scene 1

On stage: In the forest clearing — materials for building the Wendy house
Cluster of red-spotted mushrooms with one large and prominent

Personal: **Tootles and Nibs**: bows and arrows
Tootles: detachable sole of shoe
The other boys: knives in their belts
Starkey and some of the Pirates: pistols
Smee: spectacles
Hook: double cigar-holder, iron hook, sedan chair
Wendy: acorn button
John: top hat

Scene 2

On stage: Dinghy

Personal: **Tiger Lily**: bonds
Peter: sword
Smee: cutlass, lantern

Starkey: lantern
Hook: sword

SCENE 3

On stage: As before

SCENE 4

On stage: Totem pole
Dressing as desired

Personal: **Indians**: pipes

SCENE 5

On stage: In the underground hideout — curtained chamber for **Tinker Bell,**
material, needle, thread, medicine and half a coconut shell, knapsacks on sticks

Off stage: Tom-tom **(Pirate)**

Personal: **Hook**: phial of liquid

ACT III

SCENE 1

On stage: Sewing machine
Torn sail
Lantern

Off stage: Knives, swords, bows and arrows **(Lost Boys)**
Iron hook **(Stage Management)**

Personal: **Peter**: alarm clock
Pirates: swords, cutlasses
Wendy: large cloak

SCENE 2

On stage: In the underground hideout — as before

SCENE 3

On stage: As Act I, SCENE 1 with in addition, a rocking chair

Personal: **Mr Darling**: bowler hat, umbrella
Nana: the children's night-clothes

LIGHTING PLOT

Practical fittings required: gas lamps
Various interior and exterior settings

ACT I

To open: Warm glow from the gas lamps

Cue 1   **Mrs Darling** turns down the gas lamps   (Page 8)
           Lower lighting level

Cue 2   **Wendy** goes back to bed and falls asleep   (Page 9)
           *A small beam of light — **Tink** — dances through*
           the window, dashes around the room, then disappears
           into a jug on the mantelpiece

Cue 3   **Peter**: "... where they put my shadow?"   (Page 10)
           Tink's *light comes out of the jug and gets shut in the drawer*

Cue 4   **Wendy** sews on the shadow   (Page 11)
           Lighting change to produce a large shadow on the wall

Cue 5   **Peter** opens a drawer   (Page 14)
           Tink's *light flies out and about the room*

Cue 6   **Peter**: "They hardly ever stand still."   (Page 14)
           Tink's *light disappears into the bathroom*

Cue 7   **Peter**: "Funny! Now shall I give you a thimble?"   (Page 15)
           Tink's *light appears from the bathroom*

Cue 8   **Peter**: "Simple. Watch!"   (Page 19)
           *Black-out and Spot, possibly ultra violet, on **Peter***

Cue 9   **Michael**: "Ooh ... I feel all funny ... Wooaah!"   (Page 19)
           *As Cue 8, on **Michael***

Cue 10   The orchestra strikes up "Come Away"   (Page 19)
           As Cue 8, on each of the children

Cue 11   **Peter** beckons the children to follow him   (Page 20)
           As Cue 8, on each of the children

Cue 12   As each of the children fly through the window   (Page 20)
           Fade to black-out

Cues for Alternative Ending

Cue 8	The **Darlings'** nursery vanishes	(Page 23)
	Cross-fade to sky lighting	
Cue 9	**Peter** and the children fly away	(Page 23)
	Black-out	

ACT II, SCENE 1

To open: Exterior daylight effect in the forest clearing

Cue 13	**Curly**: "See it comes. How white it is."	(Page 29)
	Tink*'s light appears*	
Cue 14	**Peter** disappears inside	(Page 34)
	Fade to black-out	

ACT II, SCENE 2

To open: Sunset. Light effects create the illusion of rippling water around the "Marooner's Rock"

Cue 15	**Wendy** holds on to **Peter**, terrified, as the CURTAIN falls	(Page 40)
	Fade to black-out	

ACT II, SCENE 3

To open: As before

Cue 16	"The Crocodile's Tune" plays	(Page 41)
	Lights fade	

ACT II, SCENE 4

To open: Sombre exterior lighting

Cue 17	The war dance continues	(Page 43)
	Lights flash	
Cue 18	Climax of war dance	(Page 43)
	Black-out	

ACT II, SCENE 5

To open: Semi-darkness in the forest clearing.
Early evening interior light in the underground hideout

Cue 19   **Wendy** picks up a needle and thread and begins to sew   (Page 43)
              Lights dim on the underground hideout and come up
                  on the forest clearing

Cue 20   **Peter** makes his way towards the tree trunk entrance   (Page 44)
              Lights fade on the clearing and come up
                  in the underground hideout

Cue 21   **Peter** and **Tiger Lily** enter the forest clearing   (Page 46)
              Lights come up on the forest clearing

Cue 22   **Peter** returns to the underground hideout   (Page 47)
              Lights fade on the clearing

Cue 23   **Peter** "Get back, all of you."   (Page 48)
              Lights come up in the forest clearing

Cue 24   The children are dragged off   (Page 49)
              Lights dim in the forest clearing

Cue 25   **Peter** stirs. Soft jingling from **Tink** can be heard   (Page 52)
              Tink's *light hovers near* **Peter**. *As the jingling grows*
                  fainter through the ensuing scene, so **Tink**'s *light fades too*

Cue 26   The adults in the audience are encourage to shout   (Page 54)
              Tink's *light shines a little brighter*

Cue 27   **Peter**: " ... SAVE HER!!" Audiences stamp and clap   (Page 54)
              Tinkerbell's *light slowly becomes a little brighter*

Cue 28   The music stops abruptly   (Page 55)
              The stage darkens. Tink's light is still very faint

Cue 29   The jingling becomes louder   (Page 55)
              The beam of light grows stronger to full strength.
              The beam of light dances around the stage

Cue 30   **Peter** bounds into the auditorium   (Page 55)
              Bring up house lights. Bring up flashing and colourful lights

Cue 31   Music 29: Instrumental   (Page 55)
              Fade to black-out

ACT III, Scene 1

To open: Exterior daylight

Cue 32   There is a cheer from the boys   (Page 61)
             Fade to black-out

ACT III, Scene 2

To open: Exterior lighting

Cue 33   **Wendy** and **John** exit   (Page 63)
             Tink'*s light appears*

Cue 34   **Peter:** "Hurry!"   (Page 64)
             Tink'*s light follows* **Peter** *out*

Cue 35   **Tink** jingles and follows **Peter** out   (Page 64)
             Black-out

ACT III, Scene 3

To open: Warm glow from gas lamps

Cue 36   **Mr Darling** snuggles into **Nana**'s kennel   (Page 65)
             The stage darkens

Cue 37   **Peter Pan** flies into the room   (Page 65)
             Tink'*s light hovers near* **Peter** *throughout the ensuing action*

Cue 38   Music 37: Instrumental   (Page 66)
             Tink'*s light flies off*

Cue 39   **Peter** and **Tinker Bell** fly off into the night   (Page 66)
             Lights come up

Cue 40   Music 40: Don't Say Goodbye   (Page 71)
             Fade to black-out

EFFECTS PLOT

ACT I

Cue 1 **Wendy** goes back to bed (Page 9)
Soft jingle of bells, disappearing into the jug

Cue 2 **Peter**: "...where they put my shadow?" (Page 10)
Jingle

Cue 3 **Peter**: "You can't hear her, can you?" (Page 14)
Muffled jingle

Cue 4 **Peter** opens a drawer (Page 14)
Loud jingle

Cue 5 **Peter**: " ... you shouldn't say such things." (Page 14)
Soft jingle

Cue 6 **Peter**: "... know you were in there?" (Page 14)
Soft jingle

Cue 7 **Peter**: "... so naughty before." (Page 15)
Soft jingle

Cue 8 **Peter**: "Why, Tink?" (Page 15)
Soft jingle

ACT II

Cue 9 **Hook**: "Ay, that's the fear that haunts me." (Page 27)
Smoke begins to rise from the mushroom

Cue 10 The **Pirates** lift the mushroom top (Page 28)
Smoke pours fourth from the fourth

Cue 11 **Hook**: "When I give the order, you —— " (Page 28)
Loud ticking. Continue until crocodile exits

Cue 12 **Curly**: "How white it is!" (Page 29)
Shrill jingle

Cue 13   **Slightly**: "Hallo, Tink!"   (Page 29)
          Jingle

Cue 14   **Slightly**: "What!"   (Page 29)
          Jingle

Cue 15   **Slightly**: "Ay, that's a kiss."   (Page 31)
          Soft jingle

Cue 16   **Peter:** "Be gone from me forever."   (Page 31)
          Soft jingle

Cue 17   **Peter** snatches **John**'s top hat, knocks out the bottom   (Page 33)
          and puts the hat on the roof
          The hat begins to smoke gently

Cue 18   To open SCENE 2   (Page 35)
          Dry ice creating the illusion of rippling water

Cue 19   **Peter** "throws" his voice across the water, imitating **Hook** (Page 36)
          Throwing voice across water effect
          See dialogue pp36-39

Cue 20   **Starkey**: "Slowly."   (Page 39)
          Crocodile ticking

Cue 21   **The crocodile** follows the boat off   (Page 40)
          Ticking fades

Cue 22   **Wendy**: "No!"   (Page 40)
          Sound of waves

Cue 23   To open SCENE 3   (Page 40)
          Dry ice creating the impression of a high tide

Cue 24   **Peter**: "It will not be long now."   (Page 41)
          Alarm clock goes off

Cue 25   **Peter**: " — don't you, old chap?"   (Page 41)
          Crocodile burps

Cue 26   **Nibs**: "... and take Wendy on a journey."   (Page 47)
          Jingle

Cue 27   **Peter**: "... see you in your négligé."   (Page 47)
          Frantic jingle

ACT III